D0525407

The Beginner's Guide to Computers and the Internet

Windows® XP Edition

by Susan Holden and Matthew Francis

SUMMERSDALE

First published in 2002
This 2nd edition published in 2004
This edition copyright © Susan Holden and Matthew Francis, 2004

Reprinted 2005

Microsoft ® and Windows ® are registered trademarks of
Microsoft Corporation. All other trademarks are acknowledged
as belonging to their respective companies.

The right of Susan Holden and Matthew Francis to be identified
as the authors of this work has been asserted in accordance
with sections 77 and 78 of the Copyright, Designs and Patents
Act 1988.

Condition of Sale
This book is sold subject to the condition that it shall not, by
way of trade or otherwise, be lent, re-sold, hired out or otherwise
circulated in any form of binding or cover other than that in
which it is published and without a similar condition including
this condition being imposed on the subsequent publisher.

Summersdale Publishers Ltd
46 West Street
Chichester
West Sussex
PO19 1RP
UK

www.summersdale.com

Printed and bound in Great Britain

ISBN 1 84024 396 1

Warning and Disclaimer

Every effort has been made to make this book as accurate as possible. The authors and publishers shall have neither responsibility nor liability to any person or entity with respect to any loss or damage arising from information contained in this book.

While every effort has been made to trace copyright holders, Summersdale Publishers apologise in advance for any unintentional omission or neglect and will be pleased to insert appropriate acknowledgement to companies or individuals in any subsequent edition of this publication.

Acknowledgements

Microsoft screenshots copyright © the Microsoft Corporation reprinted by permission. MSN, Microsoft, MS DOS, Windows, Outlook Express and Internet Explorer are registered trademarks and the Office Assistant is a character logo of the Microsoft Corporation.

Classic Gold Digital screenshot copyright © Classic Gold Digital Ltd. Classic Gold Digital logos and product and service names are the trademarks of Classic Gold Digital Ltd.

Google screenshots copyright © Google Ltd. Google logos and product and service names are the trademarks of Google Ltd.

Beagle 2 screenshots reproduced by kind permission of Dr Judith Pillinger. Copyright © Beagle 2. All Rights Reserved.

Macromedia screenshots copyright © Macromedia Inc. Macromedia logos and product and service names are the trademarks of Macromedia Inc.

Ask Jeeves screenshots copyright © Ask Jeeves Inc. Logos and product and service names are the trademarks of Ask Jeeves Inc.

directory.co.uk screenshot copyright © Shopping.net Limited.Logos and product and service names are the trademarks of directory.co.uk. All rights reserved.

AltaVista screenshots © AltaVista. AltaVista is a registered trademark and The Search Company and the AltaVista logo are trademarks of AltaVista Company.

HDRA is the registered trademark and logo of the HDRA – the organic organisation. Thanks to webmaster Simon Levermore for permission to reproduce pages from the HDRA web site.

The screenshot of the European Space Agency, Mars Express web site is reproduced with kind permission of the ESA.

All images used are the property of and copyright of the companies concerned. Use of the material belonging to the above mentioned companies is not meant to convey any endorsement of this book.

Thanks also to Jean and Pat who trialled some of the material within this book.

Dedicated to

IFR
and
Shirley and Jim

Courage mounteth upon occasion

Introduction

This book seeks to introduce the reader to some of the basic elements of Windows XP and makes the assumption that the reader has no prior knowledge of computing. It uses everyday language and aims to describe procedures and terms in the simplest way possible. The emphasis is on action and success without wasting time in long technical explanations. Each chapter is divided into sections that contain essential information about each topic. These are followed by a series of actions designed to lead to success in the reader's journey to computer competence.

These easy steps introduce and develop some of the most useful areas of the computer, including the Internet and e-mail, how to stay in control of your PC and how to keep it healthy. It also covers the basic and most common word processing elements needed to produce documents. A Jargon Buster is included at the back of the book to explain any unfamiliar terms.

Chapter One:
How to Get Started

Section 1: Switching On...13
Section 2: The Desktop..14
Section 3: Icons...15
Section 4: The Mouse...15
Section 5: Clicking..16
Section 6: Pointers...18
Section 7: Exploring the Start Menu..18
Section 8: Introducing the Keyboard...20
Section 9: Introducing Windows..21
Section 10: Moving a Window Using the Title Bar...................................23
Section 11: Minimising, Maximising, Restoring and Closing...................24
Section 12: Introducing Menus...26
Section 13: Introducing Dialogue Boxes..28
Section 14: Customising your Clicking Speed..31
Section 15: Opening a Program..33
Section 16: Mouse Control and Solitaire...35
Section 17: Shutting down...39

Chapter Two:
How to use Microsoft Word

Section 1: Creating Documents – Word Processing.................................42
Section 2: The Word Window and its Features..44
Section 3: Minimise Maximise and Restore..47
Section 4: Moving Around the Page Using the Keyboard Features........50
Section 5: Creating Text, Deleting and the I-Beam..................................53
Section 6: Capitals, 'Caps Lock' and the Shift Key....................................55
Section 7: Highlighting Text..55
Section 8: Using the Tab and Cursor Keys...57
Section 9: The Formatting Toolbar and Font Boxes..................................58
Section 10: Bold, Italic and Underline Buttons...61
Section 11: Alignment and Justify...63
Section 12: Changing the Colour of Text...65
Section 13: Undo and Redo...67
Section 14: Spelling and Grammar..69
Section 15: Moving Text...72
Section 16: Copying Between Documents...74

Section 17: The Menu Bar...75
Section 18: Opening a New Document..76
Section 19: Saving a Document...79
Section 20: Saving to a Floppy Disk..83
Section 21: Opening a Document from My Documents....................85
Section 22: Opening a Document from Floppy Disk.........................87
Section 23: Margins..89
Section 24: Print Preview...91
Section 25: Toolbars..95
Section 26: Headers and Footers..98
Section 27: Viewing the Page..101
Section 28: The Ruler..103
Section 29: Line Spacing...103
Section 30: Bullets and Numbering...107
Section 31: Find and Replace..111
Section 32: Inserting Symbols...113
Section 33: Inserting a Picture..114
Section 34: Shortcuts..116
Section 35: Word Templates and Wizards..119

Chapter Three:
How to use Help

Section 1: Help on Windows XP..122
Section 2: Finding the Help and Support Center.............................122
Section 3: Using the Help and Support Center................................124
Section 4: Help and Support Center Search Box..............................129
Section 5: What's This? On Dialogue Boxes....................................130
Section 6: What's This? On Microsoft Word....................................133
Section 7: Word Processing and the Office Assistant.......................134
Section 8: Show or Hide the Office Assistant..................................136
Section 9: Changing the Office Assistant...137
Section 10: Microsoft Word Help..139
Section 11: Microsoft Works Help...141
Section 12: Microsoft Help on the Web 143

Chapter Four:
How to Play Computer Games

Section 1: Computer Games and your PC..144

Section 2: Standard Microsoft Games..145
Section 3: Games on CD or DVD...150
Section 4: Games on the Internet and Game Developers.......................152
Section 5: Games Magazines..154
Section 6: Have a Go Before you Buy..154

Chapter Five:
How to Use Disks, Play Music and Watch Movies

Section 1: Types of Disks..155
Section 2: How to Load and Eject a Floppy Disk...............................157
Section 3: How to Insert, Eject and Autorun a CD-ROM or DVD.....158
Section 4: CD-ROM that does not Autorun..159
Section 5: Loading and Running Computer Games on CD..................161
Section 6: Copying Files and Folders onto CD-R or CD-RW..............161

Chapter Six:
How to Stay in Control of Your PC

Section 1: The Control Panel..168
Section 2: Desktop Styles...172
Section 3: Customising the Desktop...175
Section 4: The Screen Saver...177
Section 5: Customising the Screen Saver..180
Section 6: Appearance and Themes: Styles, Fonts and Colour.............181
Section 7: Moving and Hiding the Taskbar..184
Section 8: Customising the Start Menu...186
Section 9: Sounds and Audio Devices: Volume Control......................190
Section 10: Volume Control...193
Section 11: The Mouse..196
Section 12: Mouse Wheels...197
Section 13: Customising the Pointer...199
Section 14: Altering the Date and Time..202
Section 15: Altering the Time Zone..203
Section 16: Keyboard Properties..205
Section 17: Adding a Program..207
Section 18: Removing a Program..209
Section 19: Viewing Fonts...211
Section 20: Using Search..213

Section 21: Creating Shortcuts...217
Section 22: Removing Shortcuts from your Desktop................................222

Chapter Seven:
How to Create and Manage Files

Section 1: Finding Windows Explorer through My Computer.....................224
Section 2: Looking at Folders..229
Section 3: Viewing Folders and Files on a Disk.................................230
Section 4: Viewing Options for Files and Folders..............................231
Section 5: Creating and Naming Folders..232
Section 6: Renaming a File or Folder..234
Section 7: Creating a Shortcut..236
Section 8: Copying a File or Folder...237
Section 9: Moving Files into a Folder...238
Section 10: Lost Files..239
Section 11: Using the Right Mouse Button......................................239
Section 12: Deleting Files..241
Section 13: Deleting Files or Folders from a Floppy Disk......................242
Section 14: The Recycle Bin...243
Section 15: My Documents Window: File and Folder Tasks........................245
Section 16: Creating a New Folder...247
Section 17: Moving a Folder...248
Section 18: Copying a Folder..249
Section 19: Deleting a Folder...250

Chapter Eight:
How to Get Connected to the Internet

Section 1: The Internet Explained...251
Section 2: What Sort of Computer Do I Need to Access the Internet?............251
Section 3: Connecting to the Internet...253
Section 4: Installing a Modem...254
Section 5: Detecting a Modem..255
Section 6: Detecting and Installing a Modem Automatically.....................256
Section 7: Detecting and Installing a Modem Manually..........................259
Section 8: Internet Service Provider..261
Section 9: Contacting an IAP/ISP..265
Section 10: Signing Up..267
Section 11: Logging On..269

Section 12: Disconnecting..273
Section 13: Making the Connection Icon Visible 274

Chapter Nine:
How to Use the World Wide Web

Section 1: What is the World Wide Web?..........................277
Section 2: Getting onto the Web.......................................278
Section 3: Internet Explorer..279
Section 4: Web Addresses and the Address Bar...............283
Section 5: Layout of the Web Page..................................285
Section 6: How to Spot a Link...288
Section 7: Browsing the Web...288
Section 8: Your Favorites List...289
Section 9: Creating a New Folder for Your Favorites.......291
Section 10: Renaming, Moving and Deleting Folders........292
Section 11: Favorites on the Menu Bar............................294
Section 12: Searching the Web..295
Section 13: Single Country Search...................................298
Section 14: Searching Using Keywords.............................301
Section 15: Searching for a Specific Phrase.....................303
Section 16: Safety and Security on the Internet...............304
Section 17: Internet Privacy Levels.................................306
Section 18: Firewall Protection.......................................308
Section 19: Internet Chat...311
Section 20: A Selection of Web Sites...............................313

Chapter Ten:
How to Use E-mail and Outlook
Express

Section 1: Your E-mail Program......................................319
Section 2: E-mail Addresses...320
Section 3: Setting up Outlook Express.............................322
Section 4: Opening Outlook Express................................323
Section 5: The E-mail Window..324
Section 6: The Folders List...325
Section 7: Reading an E-mail..326
Section 8: Writing a New Message...................................328
Section 9: Sending and Receiving an E-mail......................329

Section 10: Replying to an E-mail...331
Section 11: Customising the Layout of the E-mail Window........................332
Section 12: Customising E-mail...335
Section 13: Deleting...337
Section 14: Attaching Documents or Files..338
Section 15: Opening an Attachment..340
Section 16: Sending Messages to Several People 341
Section 17: Address Book...342
Section 18: Adding an Address Manually...343
Section 19: Using the Address Book for a New Message 346
Section 20: Managing and Moving Messages..348
Section 21: Blocking Unwanted E-mails..350
Section 22: E-mail Etiquette...353

Chapter Eleven:
How to Keep your Computer Healthy

Section 1: Staying Dust Free...355
Section 2: Tidiness...356
Section 3: How to Escape or Close Down...357
Section 4: What is a Computer Virus?...359
Section 5: Preventing Virus Infection..359
Section 6: Anti-Virus Software..361
Section 7: System Restore..363
Section 8: Disk Space...367
Section 9: Disk Cleanup..369
Section 10: ScanDisk: Finding and Fixing Errors.......................................371
Section 11: Defragmenting..372

Chapter Twelve:
How to Use Windows Media Player

Section 1: Windows Media Player..378
Section 2: Control Buttons..379
Section 3: Playing a Music CD...380
Section 4: Tuning into a Radio Station...381
Section 5: Viewing a Webcast...384
Section 6: Choosing a Skin...387
Section 7: Visualizations...389
Section 8: More about Windows Media Player...391

Chapter Thirteen:
How to Add a Scanner and a Digital Camera

Section 1: Setting up a Scanner...394
Section 2: Setting up a Digital Camera..394
Section 3: Scanner and Camera Software.......................................395
Section 4: The Scanner and Camera Installation Wizard................395

Chapter Fourteen:
How to Add a Printer and Printing

Section 1: Plug and Play...400
Section 2: Automatic Detection with the Add Printer Wizard.........400
Section 3: Manual Detection with the Add Printer Wizard.............404
Section 4: Installing a New Printer Not Listed on the Wizard.........410
Section 5: Preparing to Print..411
Section 6: Printing...414
Section 7: Printing from Outlook Express or Internet Explorer......417

Chapter Fifteen:
More on Windows

Section 1: Windows XP Tour...419
Section 2: Windows XP Interactive Training..................................421
Section 3: Calculator..424
Section 4: Accessibility Options..426

Jargon Busters...429

Chapter One:
How to Get Started

Section 1:
Switching On

Essential Information

Check that all the leads of your setup are connected. Many computers have cables and terminals, which are colour-coded to make them easy to use.

If you are uncertain about the connections, get someone experienced or a computer engineer to check them out for you. It might be a good idea to ask them to colour-code the connections for future reference.

Action 1

Locate the switch on the **monitor** (like the switch on a television, under the screen) and the **systems unit** (the rectangular box with slots for disks) and press each one to switch on. Wait while the computer starts or 'boots up'.

As the computer 'boots up' the monitor will show a black screen, with systems details showing in white text. Allow the computer to continue this process without interference.

Eventually the monitor will display the **Microsoft Windows** symbol. This will then give way to what is called the **desktop.**

Section 2:
The Desktop

Essential Information

The **desktop** (Fig. 1) is a background that houses small pictures called **icons.**

The **taskbar** is a blue strip that is usually positioned across the bottom of the screen. The **Start** button sits on one end of the taskbar and the computer clock at the other.

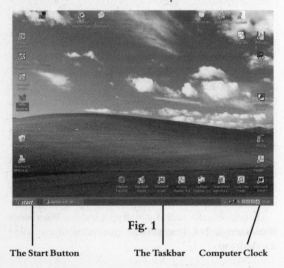

Fig. 1

The Start Button   The Taskbar   Computer Clock

The desktop provides a springboard to enter the various programs on your computer.

Section 3:
Icons

The **icons** are designed to give you a clue about the program that they are meant to represent. For example, a picture of a waste bin represents the Recycle Bin (Fig. 2) which is where you can send any unwanted items or documents.

Recycle Bin   Internet Explorer   Outlook Expre...   Microsoft Word

Fig. 2: Some desktop icons

Icons are shortcuts that have been created to lead straight into a program, activity or even a document that you have created. Each different picture represents a unique program or item on your computer. Later you will discover how to create these shortcuts yourself.

Section 4:
The Mouse

Essential Information

The mouse will have two (sometimes three) buttons on the top and a ball set in the underside. Some models also have a small wheel on the top. This is used for scrolling – more about this later.

Uses of the mouse:

1. Moves a pointer on the screen.
2. By moving the pointer and clicking on the left button various functions can be performed on the screen.
3. By using the right mouse button in conjunction with the pointer more complicated functions can be performed.

Action 1

Place the palm of your writing hand lightly over the body of the mouse. Your fingers should be resting over buttons. Move the mouse forward and backward on the mouse mat so that the ball on the underside is moved. (A mouse mat creates friction between the mouse ball and the surface, allowing it to operate efficiently.)

Action 2

Once again, move the mouse and see how the pointer moves across the desktop on the computer screen. Notice that the pointer at this stage is in the shape of an arrow. The arrow on the screen moves in the same direction as the mouse.

Section 5:
Clicking

Essential Information

There are two types of clicking: single and double.

Action 1

Place the forefinger of your writing hand over the *left* mouse button and press once. This is a single click. Now press twice in rapid succession. This is called a double click.

Practise double-clicking as it does take some people a considerable time to get the hang of it. Do not be concerned if you find this difficult as the computer can be adjusted to your speed (Section 14).

Top Tip

There is an alternative if you have problems with double-clicking. When instructions call for a double click, use a single click and then press the Enter key.

Action 2

The click and drag technique is used to move objects or text.

Move the pointer onto the **My Computer** icon. Click once on the left-hand button and hold your finger down. Do not release. Whilst the button remains depressed, move the pointer across the screen, and if you are doing it correctly you will also move the icon. Release the button and the icon will stay in the new position.

Now try moving the other icons across the screen. Release them and then move them back again.

Top Tip

Be neat – Leave your desktop looking tidy!

Section 6:
Pointers

The pointer will change shape according to the task that it is performing. Figure 3 shows the shapes that you will encounter in this section of the book. The appearance of the egg timer means that you need to wait for a task to be completed.

normal arrow   **working**   **busy pointer**

Fig. 3

When the computer has finished performing a task, the pointer will return to the normal arrow shape.

Section 7:
Exploring the Start Menu

Essential Information
The **Start Menu** is a point of access to many of the programs and facilities on the computer.

Action 1
Move your pointer onto the Start button, and click once. A menu appears similar to the one in Figure 4. Take a moment to familiarise yourself with the layout. When you have finished, move your pointer away from the Start menu

and onto the desktop. Click once and the menu will disappear.

The Internet and e-mail programs

The folders where you will keep most of your work

A list of your most frequently used programs. Click on an icon to go straight to the program

Shortcuts to other sections of your PC

Click on All Programs for a complete list

Fig. 4: Buttons which enable you to Log Off or Turn Off computer

Section 8:
Introducing the Keyboard

Essential Information

Computer keyboards vary greatly but they do all contain the same functions - it's just a case of locating them. The main groups of keys are shown in Figure 5.

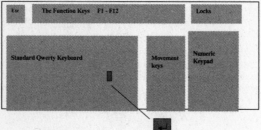

Fig. 5

Fig. 6: Return/Enter

Action 1

Locate the **Enter** key. This may be of various shapes but it will probably have an arrow on it like the one in Figure 6. Some keyboards have the words 'Return' or 'Enter' written on the key.

This key has a number of uses but in this section it will be used to help open various programs on the computer. For the moment, just be aware of the name and location of this important key. You will meet other uses for it later on.

Section 9:
Introducing Windows

Essential Information

A **window** shows what is contained within a program
which is represented by an icon. For example on the desktop
is the **Recycle Bin**. Imagine that it is an ordinary waste
bin where you put your rubbish. If you open the Recycle
Bin by double-clicking on the icon, a window appears
displaying the contents.

Action 1

Move the pointer onto the Recycle Bin icon (Fig. 7) and
click once.

Recycle
Bin

Fig. 7

Press **Enter** on your keyboard. A window opens as in
Figure 8.

Window sizing buttons and close box

Title bar

Menu bar

Window border

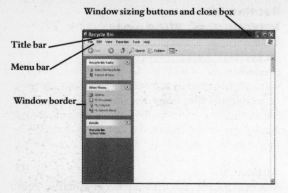

Fig. 8

At the moment the Recycle Bin is empty, hence the blank window.

Action 2

Look at the following features of the window in Figure 8. All the windows have them.

1. The edges are defined by the **window border**.
2. Along the top of the window is a **title bar** which is used for moving the window.
3. In the top right hand corner are the **sizing buttons.**
4. Next to the sizing buttons is the **Close Box** (denoted by a cross).

22

Section 10:
Moving a Window Using the Title Bar

Action 1

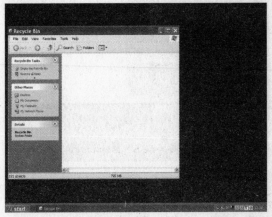

Fig. 9

Move the mouse cursor onto the Recycle Bin title bar (aim for the name of the window, i.e. Recycle Bin), click the left-hand mouse button and hold it down.

Action 2

Fig. 10

Drag the mouse across the mouse mat and at the same time the Recycle Bin window will be dragged across the screen . Release the mouse button and the window will stay in its new position.

Section 11:
Minimising, Maximising, Restoring and Closing

Essential Information
These are functions that alter the size of windows and

documents, enabling you to work on several at once. They are known as sizing buttons and are present on all windows, dialogue boxes and documents, so do take a little time to become comfortable using them.

minimise maximise close

Recycle Bin

File Edit View Favorites Tools Help

Back · ⊙ · 🗇 · 🔎 Search 📁 Folders 📖 ▾

Recycle Bin Tasks

Fig. 11

Action 1
Click on the **maximise** button and the Recycle Bin window will fill the whole screen.

Action 2
Notice that the maximise button has now changed to the **restore** button.

restore

Fig. 12

Action 3
Click on the restore button and the window will return to its original size.

Action 4

Click on the minimise button and the window will shrink to a button on the taskbar.

Recycle Bin button

Fig. 13

Action 5

Click on the Recycle Bin button on the taskbar and the window will return to the screen.

Action 6

Click on the **Close** button and the window will close.

Section 12:
Introducing Menus

Essential Information

Once again, open the Recycle Bin by double-clicking on the desktop icon (or single-click and press Enter). Along the top of the window, below the title bar is a row of words on a grey strip. This is called the **menu bar** (Fig. 14). Menus are found on windows and some boxes. They give access to the facilities of the program.

Fig. 14

Action 1

Move the pointer onto the Recycle Bin icon and double-click (or single-click and press Enter).

Action 2

Move the pointer to **View** on the menu bar, and click once. A box appears below the View option (Fig. 15). This list of words is a **menu**.

To remove it, move the pointer off the menu and onto the window; click once and the menu disappears.

Action 3

Close the window by clicking on the **Close** box.

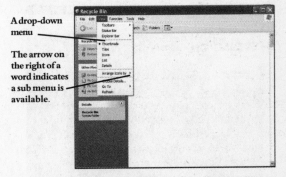

A drop-down menu

The arrow on the right of a word indicates a sub menu is available.

Fig. 15

Section 13:
Introducing Dialogue Boxes

Essential Information
Dialogue Boxes allow you to choose and select options in order to customise your computer.

Action 1
Move the pointer onto the **Start** button and click once, so that the Start menu appears. Move the pointer up to **Control Panel** and click once.

If you have followed the correct path, the Control Panel window will open (Fig. 16).

Fig. 16: Control Panel window

Action 2
Click once on **Appearance and Themes** and a new window opens (Fig. 17).

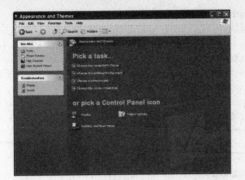

Fig. 17

Action 3

Click once on **Taskbar and Start Menu** and a dialogue box called **Taskbar and Start Menu Properties** opens (Fig. 18).

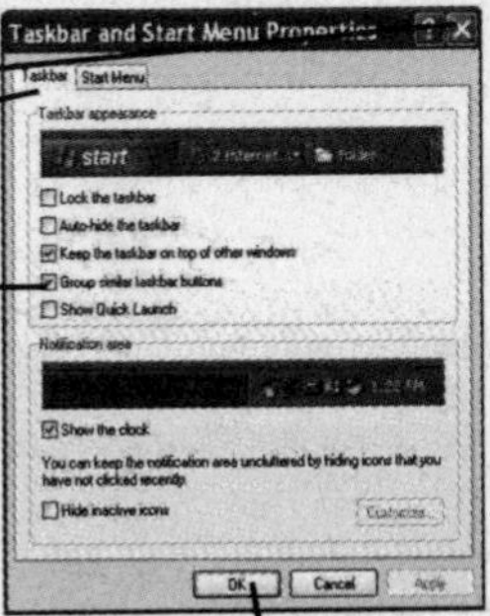

Close box

Tabs

Check boxes:
These are a way
of making a selection.
By clicking on a check
box you cause a tick to
either appear or disappear.

Fig. 18

Command Buttons: These allow
you to decide a course of action.

Action 4

Click on the check box by **Show the clock** and remove the tick. Click on the command button **Apply**. Now look on the preview bar in the **Notification Area** and you will see that the clock has been removed from the task bar. Now click on the check box to reinstate the tick, click **Apply** and the clock will re-appear on both the preview bar and the task bar. Clicking **OK** on the dialogue box would confirm your selection but on this occasion there is no need to do this.

Action 5

Locate the tabs at the top of the dialogue box and click once on the tab called **Start Menu.** The Start menu properties are displayed (Fig. 19), showing **radio buttons.** These allow you to choose between various options. Once you have made your selection, you will need to click on the command button **Apply** and then **OK** in order to confirm. On this occasion however, close the dialogue box by clicking on the Close box in the top right-hand corner.

Radio Buttons:
These are circles with dots in the centre. By clicking on a circle you cause a dot to either appear or disappear. This is a method used for selecting options.

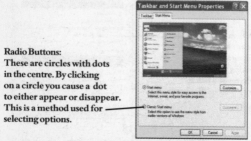

Fig. 19

Section 14:
Customising your Clicking Speed

Essential Information

The computer has got to be able to recognise the difference between a single click and a double click. If your double click is too slow it will appear to the computer as two single clicks. We all click at different speeds. In response to this your Microsoft Application has been designed to allow you to customise the computer to respond to a clicking speed that is comfortable for you. To do this you need first to go to **Mouse Properties**.

Action 1

Click on the Start button and then on Control Panel. Move the mouse pointer onto **Printers and Other Hardware**. Click once.

The **Printers and Other Hardware** window opens (Fig. 20). Move the pointer onto **Mouse**. Click once and you will open **Mouse Properties** (Fig. 21).

Fig. 20

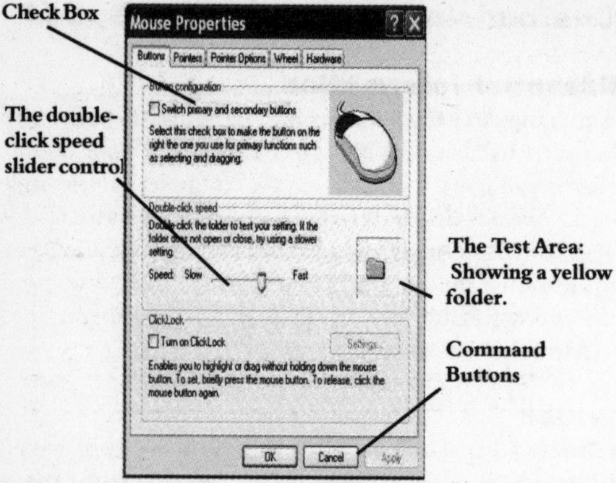

Check Box

Mouse Properties

The double-click speed slider control

The Test Area:
Showing a yellow folder.

Command Buttons

Fig. 21

Action 2

To test your clicking speed, move the pointer onto the test area. Try double-clicking on the yellow folder. If your clicking speed corresponds to the current double-click speed setting, the folder will open. Double-click again and the folder will close.

If you cannot open or close the folder, the double-click speed can be reduced. Follow Action 3.

Action 3

Place the pointer on the slider control, depress the left button, hold it down and drag the slider towards **Slow**.

Retest your double-click speed on the yellow folder and adjust the slider control until you achieve a double-click that opens the folder.

Once you are happy with the adjustment click on the command button **Apply** and the computer will set itself at that speed. To close the Mouse Properties dialogue box, click on **OK.**

Top Tip

If you are left-handed and wish to reconfigure the mouse to a left-handed option, Chapter 6 Section 11 will give you directions.

Action 4

To close the Printers and Other Hardware window click once on the Close box.

Section 15:
Opening a Program

Essential Information

A program can be opened through an icon on the desktop or by going to the **Start** menu and **All Programs.**

Action 1

Choose an icon on your desktop, any one will do. They all represent programs. Open your chosen program by either double-clicking on the icon or by a single click and then pressing **Enter**. Close the program by clicking on the Close box.

Action 2

Click on the Start button and move the pointer onto **All Programs** (Fig. 22). Another menu appears showing all the programs listed on your computer .

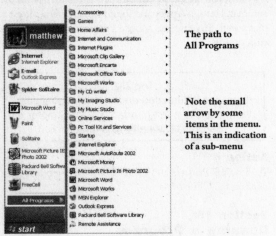

The path to All Programs

Note the small arrow by some items in the menu. This is an indication of a sub-menu

Fig. 22

Choose a program without a sub menu and click once. The program will open. Close the program by clicking on the Close box.

Section 16:
Mouse Control and Solitaire

Essential Information
The game of Solitaire is very useful for practising mouse control, clicking and dragging. Solitaire is also known as Patience.

Action 1
Go to Start and click once. Click on **All Programs**, **Games** and then **Solitaire**. This path is shown in Fig. 23.

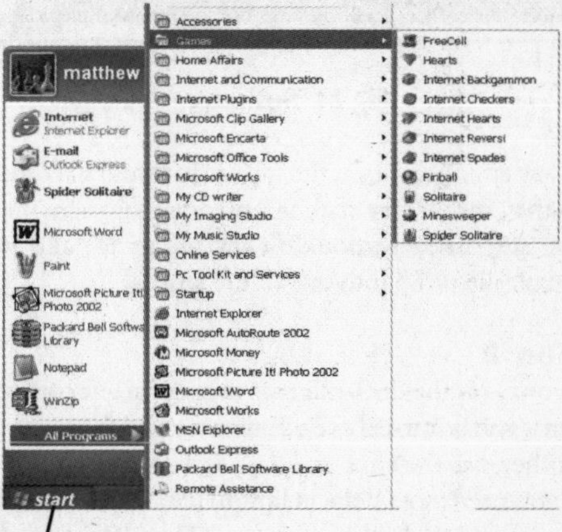

Start Button

Fig. 23: Path to Games and Solitaire

When you reach Solitaire, click once and Solitaire opens.

Fig 24: Solitaire

The four empty spaces at the top are to house the four aces when they appear. Try clicking and dragging them into the spaces. Alternatively, double-click on an ace and it will automatically jump into one of the spaces.

Action 2

Click once on the deck of cards in the top left corner and the cards will be turned over. To move a card from one place to another, use the click and drag technique.

If you need more help on how to play Patience/Solitaire click on the **Help** button at the top. The Help drop-down menu opens (Fig. 25).

How to get Started

Help button   Help drop-down menu

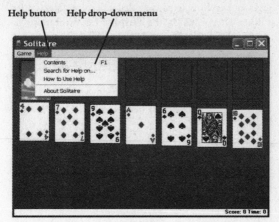

Fig. 25

Action 3

Click once on **Contents**, which then opens (Fig. 26).

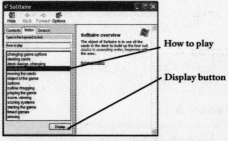

Fig. 26: Solitaire overview

Click once on **how to play** so that it becomes highlighted in blue. Then click on the **Display** button. Details on how **To play Solitaire** are displayed (Fig. 27).

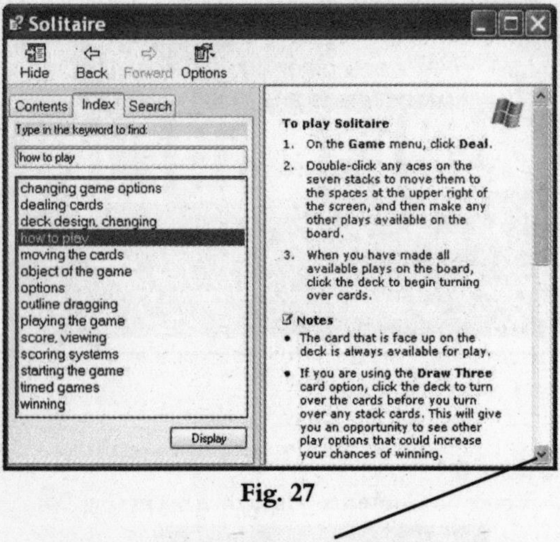

Fig. 27

Click continuously on this arrow and the text will scroll thus enabling you to read more of the text on display.

Action 4

To remove Display, click on the Close box. You will be returned back to Solitaire.

Action 5

When you have finished playing the game, close it down by clicking on the Close box.

Top Tip
You're probably keen to conquer your computer
and consequently regard playing Solitaire as a
waste of time. It really isn't: it's a valuable lesson in
mouse control and other techniques so do spare
some time and have a go!

Section 17:
Shutting Down

Essential Information
There is a set procedure to follow in order to safely to shut
down your computer.
Before you shut down, always close any windows still open
by clicking once on the close box of each window. You
should then be looking at the desktop.

Action 1
Click once on **Start** with the pointer. Highlight **Turn off
Computer.** Click once (Fig. 28).

Fig. 28

The **Turn off computer** box appears (Fig. 29).

Fig. 29

Action 2

Click on the **Turn Off** button. The computer will close down its program and automatically switch itself off.

Should you change your mind and not wish to turn off the computer, click on the Cancel button.

Chapter Two:
How to use Microsoft Word

Section 1:
Creating Documents – Word Processing

Essential Information

The word processing program contains text formatting tools, characters, numbers, styles and designs which you can use to create a wide range of professional looking documents. This chapter gives a brief introduction to some of the many things that you can do on Microsoft Word. To further expand your knowledge or if you have any difficulties while using Word, try using the Help button, the Office Assistant or What's This? For more information, read *Chapter 3: How to Use Microsoft Help*.

To open the word processing program follow the actions below.

Action 1

Look for a shortcut icon on the desktop (Fig.1). Double-click on the icon and it will take you straight into the word processing program.

Microsoft Word

Fig. 1

Alternatively, click on the **Start** button and from the Start menu, select **Microsoft Word** (Figs. 2 and 3).

Microsoft Works

If you have Microsoft Works then open the Microsoft Works Task Launcher either by going to the **Start** menu and **All Programs** (Fig. 3) or by clicking on the **Works** icon on the desktop. Once open, click on **Programs** on the menu bar at the top and then on **Word**.

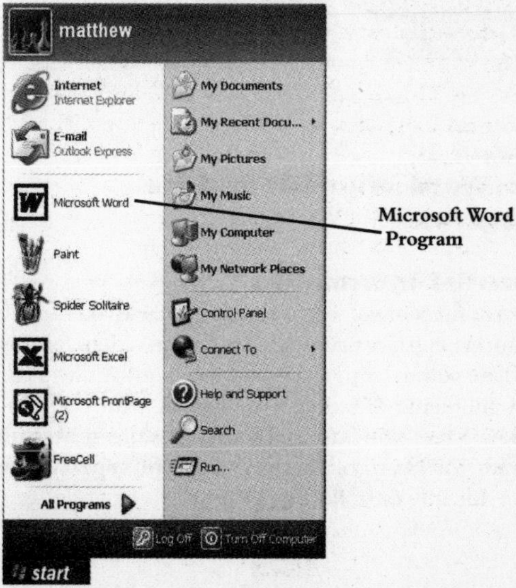

Fig. 2

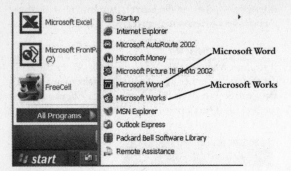

Fig. 3

Section 2:
The Word Window and its Features

Essential Information

The basic functions of word processing enable you to create documents, enhance them and save them in various formats. If you are new to word processing it is worthwhile to take a few moments to familiarise yourself with the Word window. Once you have opened your word processing program, the Microsoft Word window will appear on the screen. Identify the following features.

How to use Microsoft Word

Blue title bar   Menu bar   Toolbars   Close

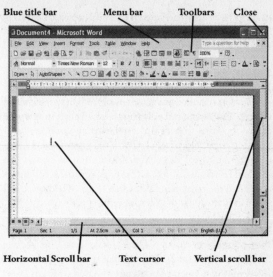

Horizontal Scroll bar   Text cursor   Vertical scroll bar

Fig. 4

Menu Bar and Toolbars

At the top of the screen is a grey strip containing a line of words from **File** to **Help**. This is called the **Menu bar.** Below this are further grey strips called **toolbars** that carry rows of small icons. Notice that there is a blinking cursor on the screen. This is the **text cursor**, which indicates where the text will appear on the screen.

Pointer and I-beam

Move the pointer over the white page and notice when it

changes from an arrow into an **I**. This shape is called an **I-beam**. Move it onto the toolbars at the top of the page and it will change to an arrow.

Scroll Bars

Look at Figure 4 and identify the **scroll bar**. This is a device that enables you to see more of the page on the screen. The screen can only show a small portion of a page at any one time. Try clicking on the upward or downward pointing arrow and you will see that the page can be scrolled vertically to reveal more of the document. It can also be scrolled horizontally, left or right. A vertical scroll bar is always on the right-hand side of the page. The horizontal scroll at is always at the bottom of the page.

Title Bar

Notice that the name of the document (Fig. 4 says 'Document 4') is on the blue title bar at the top of the page. Every time you open a document its name will be present on the title bar.

Moving the Window

If you want to move the window, click on the Microsoft Word blue title bar, hold down the *left* mouse button and drag the pointer downward towards the bottom of the screen. Release the button when about halfway across the screen. Now move the window back to its original position, using the same method of clicking and dragging the blue bar.

Section 3:
Minimise, Maximise and Restore

Essential Information

These are functions that will enable you to manipulate the pages and programs on the screen. They are used all the time in word processing so do take a little time to become comfortable using them.

In the top right-hand corner of the Microsoft Word window you will have one of these two sets of boxes (Figs. 5 and 5a):

Minimise   Restore down   Close

Fig. 5

Minimise   Maximise   Close

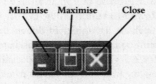

Fig. 5a

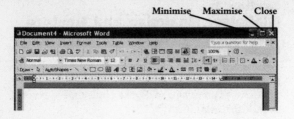

Fig. 6

Action 1

Your window may show either Figure 5 or Figure 5a. If it shows **Restore down** (Fig. 5), click on it once and watch what happens. Look closely at the centre box. It should now show **Maximise** (Fig. 5a). If so click on it once and watch what happens. Look closely at the centre box. It should now show **Restore** (Fig. 5).

Action 2

Click on the **Minimise** button and the whole window will shrink down to a button on the taskbar (Fig. 7). It is possible to open up a number of documents and then minimise them so that they sit on the taskbar and are thus easy to recall when you need them, especially during the process of copying from one document to another.

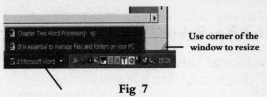

Use corner of the
window to resize

Fig 7

List of documents sitting on the taskbar

To restore the documents to the screen, simply click on the
document button on the taskbar and a list will appear.
Click on your selection.

Action 3

You can also make larger windows smaller by using the
pointer. Move the pointer to the bottom right-hand corner
of the window frame (Fig. 7) and it will change to a double-
headed arrow.

Now click on the left-hand mouse button, hold it down
and drag the pointer across the screen. As you drag the
pointer you will also drag the outside frame of the window.
Release the button when the window is the size that you
wish.

Top Tip

Click on Maximise and the window will
expand. Click on Restore and the window will
reduce down to a smaller size.

Section 4:
Moving Around the Page Using the Keyboard Features

Essential Information

The keyboard, as well as the mouse, allows you to interact with the computer and move text and the cursor around the page. If you have previously used a typewriter then you will be familiar with the layout of the traditional 'Qwerty' format. Besides having normal keyboard functions the computer keyboard can also be used to give additional commands to the word processing program. Identify the following keys on your keyboard.

Space Bar

This is in the centre of the bottom row of the keyboard and allows you to put a space between texts. If you keep pressing the space bar, the blinking text cursor will move across the page.

Top Tip
If you cannot initially see the blinking text cursor, then move the mouse pointer onto the page, click once and it should appear.

Enter Key

Fig. 8

It is sometimes called the **Return** key. In word processing, it allows you to move the text cursor down the page and to put line spaces between sentences.

Delete Key

This removes text to the **right** of the text cursor.

Fig. 9

Backspace Key

This removes letters to the **left** of the cursor.

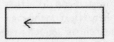

Fig. 10

Caps Lock Key

This allows you to type in capital letters.

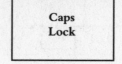

Fig. 11

Press the **Caps Lock** key (Fig. 11) once and a light comes on at the top right of your keyboard, showing that the key is activated. Press **Caps Lock** again and the light will go out.

Shift Key

This allows you to type single capital letters.

Fig. 12

Cursor Keys

These allow you to move the blinking text cursor to the top or bottom of the page and to the right or left. They will only work when there is text on the page. These keys allow you to move the text cursor about the page in the direction indicated (Fig. 13).

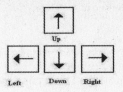

Fig. 13

The Tab Key

This key allows you to create paragraphs, columns and matching spaces in a document.

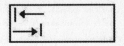

Fig. 14

Section 5:
Creating Text, Deleting and the I-Beam

Essential Information

Once the blinking text cursor is visible on the screen you can begin to type. Remember, when the pointer moves onto the white area of the page it appears as an **I-beam**.

Action 1

Make sure you are looking at a blank page. Type your name and then press **Enter**. Notice that the text cursor has moved down a line. Type the rest of your address, remembering to press Enter at the end of each line.

Action 2
If you continue to type and do not press Enter, as soon as the text cursor reaches the end of a line it will move down the page, automatically. This is called the **Wraparound** feature and it allows you to keep typing without bothering to press the Enter key in order to start a new line.

Action 3
Move the I-beam to the centre of one of the words that you have just typed, and click once with the left mouse button. Notice that the I-beam has moved the blinking text cursor to the place where you have just clicked. This is an important action in allowing you to alter and delete text.

Action 4
Move the I-beam to the centre of a word that you have typed and click once. Press the **Delete** key once and notice that a letter from the **right** of the cursor has been deleted. If you keep your finger depressed on the Delete key, the text is deleted rapidly. Repeat this procedure to delete all the text that you have just typed.

Action 5
Type a sentence on the page, leave the text cursor at the end of the sentence and then use the backspace to delete the text. Remember the backspace key removes letters to the **left** of the cursor.

Section 6:
Capitals, 'Caps Lock' and the Shift Key

Essential Information
To type capitals you can use the **Caps Lock** key or the **Shift** key.

Action 1
If you wish all of the text to be in capitals, press the **Caps Lock** key (Fig. 11) and make sure that the Caps Lock light has come on. Type the text. To return to lower case, press the **Caps Lock** key once and check the Caps Lock light has now gone out.

Action 2
You will find a **Shift** key (Fig. 12) on both sides of the keyboard. To type a single capital, press the Shift key and hold it down while you type the letter. When you release the Shift key you are returned to lower case.

Section 7:
Highlighting Text

Essential Information
Being able to highlight text is very important in producing documents. It's a very easy procedure as long as you don't move the pointer too quickly and stay off the margins.

Action 1

Type a single line of text. Place the I-beam on the same line as the text and carefully move the pointer to the left until it changes from an I-beam into an arrow. Position the pointer to the left of the text, so that the arrow points towards the words.

John Smith

If the arrow is pointing away from the text you have probably moved off the page and onto the margin. If so, move the pointer back onto the text, so that the pointer once again becomes an I-beam and try again, this time moving it more slowly and staying on the white page and on the same line as the text.

Action 2

Once you have the arrow pointing towards the text, click once on the left mouse button and the words will be highlighted.

i.e. John Smith

Action 3

Click once onto a white part of the screen and the highlight disappears.

Action 4

To highlight part of the text, place the pointer at the

beginning of the part you wish to highlight and, keeping the left mouse button depressed, move the cursor slowly over the letters.

Top Tip
It's a good idea to practise the technique of highlighting until you get the hang of it.

Action 5

It is also possible to highlight a whole document in order to make changes that apply to all of the text. Move the I-beam to the left of the text, until the I-beam changes to an arrow and is pointing towards the text. Click once on the left-hand button, hold it down and drag the arrow downwards until all of the text is highlighted. Release the left mouse button.

When the text is highlighted you can make any changes that you wish, such as changing the font style or size. Click once on the edge of the paper and the black highlight will disappear.

Section 8:
Using the Tab and Cursor Keys

Action 1

Press the **Tab** key (Fig. 14) and you will see that the text cursor moves across the screen taking bigger spaces than the space bar. To return the text cursor, press the Backspace key (Fig. 10).

Action 2

Use the Tab key to create columns like the following;

County	County Towns
Essex	Chelmsford
Dorset	Dorchester
Hertfordshire	Hertford
Oxfordshire	Oxford
Norfolk	Norwich

Section 9:
The Formatting Toolbar and Font Boxes

Essential Information

Across the top of the screen are a series of grey strips called toolbars. There are a variety of toolbars all with different names and which can be customised to appear on the screen. Move the arrow onto the icons of the toolbars. Observe that the I-beam turns into an arrow. Notice that as the arrow rests on each icon, it becomes highlighted and the name of the tool is displayed.

One toolbar allows you to format the text and alter the style of your document and is therefore called the **Formatting Toolbar** (Fig. 15).

Fig. 15

Action 1

Identify the two font boxes on the picture of the Formatting toolbar (Fig. 16).

Fig. 16

Times New Roman will normally appear as the font style because it is the **default** style set by the computer.

Jargon Buster
Default
Default means a pre-selected setting that the computer will open as first choice.

Action 2

To choose a different font, click on the black triangle (down arrow) to the right of the font box. Clicking on the down arrow (black triangle) produces a drop-down list of styles. The drop-down list also has a scroll bar; clicking on the down arrow above or below the scroll bar allows you to move up or down the list of font styles.

Font style box   Scroll bar

Fig. 17

Action 4

Move the pointer up and down the list and each font will be highlighted in turn. Select a font style that appeals to you and click once. The new style will have replaced Times New Roman as the font style.

Action 5

Font size 12 is one of the most frequently used sizes for documents. Click on the down arrow to the right of the font size box (Fig. 18). A drop-down list appears showing the font sizes.

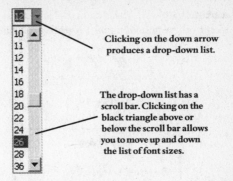

Clicking on the down arrow produces a drop-down list.

The drop-down list has a scroll bar. Clicking on the black triangle above or below the scroll bar allows you to move up and down the list of font sizes.

Fig. 18

As the pointer is moved up and down the list, each font size is highlighted in turn. Select a different size font and click once with the left mouse button to change the font size to your personal choice.

Section 10:
Bold, Italic and Underline Buttons

Essential Information

The Formatting toolbar allows you to change the appearance of text in more ways than just altering size and style. Also found on the Formatting toolbar are the **bold**, *italic* and <u>underlining</u> functions. These text formatting buttons allow you to make even more changes to your document.

Action 1

Identify these buttons on the formatting toolbar.

Fig. 19

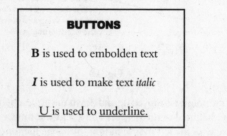

BUTTONS

B is used to embolden text

I is used to make text *italic*

U is used to <u>underline.</u>

Top Tip

To type brackets, press and hold down the Shift key at the same time as typing the bracket.

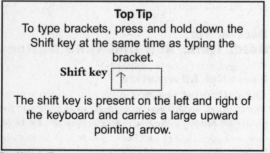

Shift key

The shift key is present on the left and right of the keyboard and carries a large upward pointing arrow.

Action 2

Type a piece of text and highlight it. Click once on the **Bold** button. Click once on the white page and the highlight disappears, showing the text emphasised in bold. Notice that the Bold button now has a blue border around the button. This shows that it is activated.

Action 3

Highlight the text. Click once on the *italic* button. Click once on the white page to remove the highlight and the whole of the text is now shown in italics.

Action 4

Highlight the text and click on the <u>underline</u> button. Now click on the white page to remove the highlight and you can see that the text is now underlined.

Action 5

To remove the Bold, Italic or Underline, highlight the text and click once on whichever button you wish to remove. Notice that the blue border around the button disappears once it has been de-activated. Click on the white page to remove the highlight.

Section 11:
Alignment and Justify

Essential information

The **Alignment** and **Justify** buttons allow you to decide on the positioning of your text on the page.

Align Left will arrange your text to the left of the page, leaving a ragged edge to the right.
Align Right will arrange the text to the right of the page.

Align Center (this is the American spelling, used by Microsoft) will arrange the text down the centre of the page.

Justify stretches the text evenly across the page.

Action 1

Identify the four alignment buttons on the formatting toolbar.

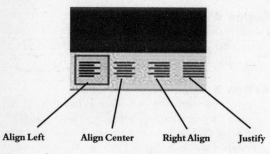

Align Left   Align Center   Right Align   Justify

Fig. 20

Action 2

Type a piece of text. Make sure that you have at least four or five lines. *Do not* press Enter. The text will probably align to the left side of the page. Check the **Align Left** button. If it is not activated, then highlight the whole of the text and click once on Align Left button. The text will then be aligned to the left of the page. Click on the page to remove the highlight. Repeat these actions using the other buttons to align right and to centre the text.

Top Tip
You can tell when a button on a toolbar is
activated because it will be outlined in blue.

Section 12:
Changing the Colour of Text

Essential Information

The formatting toolbar also allows you to change the colour
of the text, thus enabling you to produce eye-catching
documents. Of course these will only be apparent on paper
if you have a colour printer.

Action 1

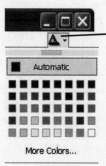

A (with black bar beneath)
on the Formatting toolbar.

Fig. 21

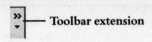 Toolbar extension

Fig. 22

Identify a button with a large letter **A** on the extreme right of the formatting toolbar (Fig. 21). You may need to click on the toolbar extension to see the font colour button (Fig. 22).

This is the font colour button. Beneath the **A** is a black bar. This indicates the current colour being used for the text. Notice the downward pointing arrow to the right of the **A**. Click once on the arrow and a drop-down colour chart is displayed. Click once on whichever colour you wish to use. The black bar beneath the **A** will change to the colour that you have selected. You can now begin typing in the new colour.

Action 2

To change the colour of existing text, highlight the section of text that you wish to change. Click on the arrow by the **Font Colour** button and click on your chosen colour from the drop-down colour chart. Click once on the page to remove the highlight and you will then be able to see the change that you have made to the text.

Section 13:
Undo and Redo

Essential Information

The Standard Toolbar (Fig. 23) like the formatting toolbar, is set at the top of the Word window. There are tools that allow you to move text, preview your work, check for mistakes and undo any mistakes.

Fig. 23

The **Undo** and **Redo** buttons can save you a great deal of time and despair! At some point you are bound to make a mistake in your typing or else delete text in error. Undo and Redo buttons will allow you to recall previous actions and text.

Action 1

Look at the Standard toolbar and identify the following:

Undo and Redo buttons

Fig. 24

Type a few lines and then delete them. Move the pointer

onto the **Undo** button. Click once and, as if by magic the text reappears.

Action 2

Move your cursor onto the **Redo** button and click once. Your line disappears again because the computer has redone your original action of deleting the first line.

Action 3

It is possible to retrieve more than just one action. Click on the downward pointing arrow by the **Undo** button. A drop-down list appears showing all your previous actions on this particular document.

Fig. 25

There is even a scroll bar to enable you to scroll back through the history of your document. You can highlight as many actions as you wish to undo and undo them in one go. The same applies to the Redo button.

<table>
<tr><td>

Top Tip
Time spent in perfecting the use of the Undo and Redo buttons will save you time and anguish later on.

</td></tr>
</table>

Section 14: Spelling and Grammar

Essential Information

Identify the **Spelling and Grammar** button (Fig. 26) on the Standard toolbar.

Fig 26

This button allows the computer to automatically check your work for spelling mistakes. However, it might not recognise personal names and places and may sometimes identify them as being incorrect.

Action 1

Type in the following but do not use all capitals. Include all spelling mistakes.

Mye lif stori begins whenn I was borrn.

As you type, a red line should appear under any word that the computer considers, to be incorrect. Any grammatical mistakes are underlined in green.

Action 2

Click on the **Spelling and Grammar** button. The Spelling and Grammar dialogue box appears, highlighting incorrect spellings in red (Fig. 27).

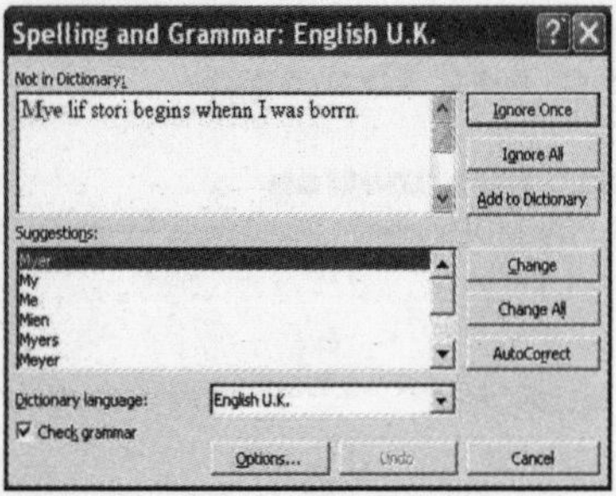

Fig. 27

You now have a choice of two ways to alter the spelling mistake.

1. In the **Suggestions** box will be a selection of alternative spellings. If you wish to use one of these alternatives, click on it, so that it is highlighted then click on **Change.**

2. If there is not a suitable alternative listed by the computer, you can correct the spelling yourself by clicking once on the word spelt wrongly and shown in red within the box. The blinking text cursor will then be in position. You are

now able to type the correct spelling. Then click on **Change.**

Action 3

If you do not wish to change the spelling at all (because it is a name or an unusual word) then click on **Ignore.** The spell-check will then continue through the document unless you click on Close. Once the spell-check has finished a message box will appear telling you that the check is complete.

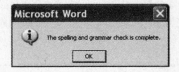

Fig. 28

Click on **OK.**

Action 4

Type this sentence: My cat wont use the cat flap.
Now click on the **Spelling and Grammar** button. The Spelling and Grammar window appears and highlights the grammatical error in green.

Action 5

In the suggestion box is an alternative 'won't'. If you wish to alter the word, then click on **Change** on the right of the window. If you do not wish to alter the word then click on **Ignore**. If you want to remove the grammar check, click once on the check box and remove the tick.

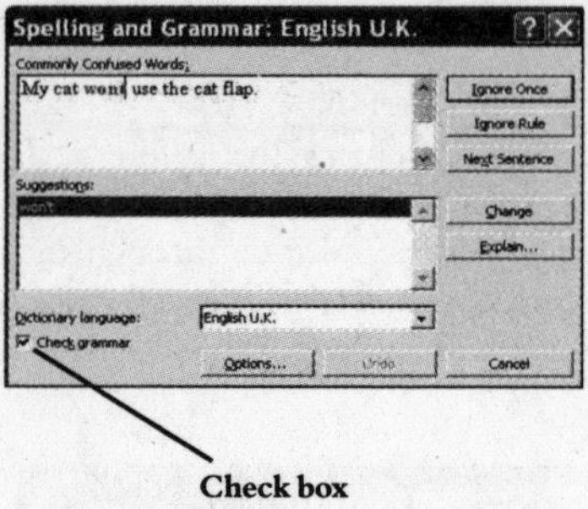

Check box

Fig. 29

Top Tip
After using the Spelling and Grammar
function, read through your document to
ensure that it still makes sense.

Section 15:
Moving text

Essential Information
The **Cut, Copy and Paste** buttons allow you to move
text to different places on the page and between documents.
Identify these functions on the **Standard Toolbar**. Move
the pointer onto each button without clicking. As it moves
onto each, a description label appears. This helps you to

select the correct button that you wish to use.

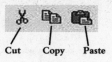

Cut   Copy   Paste

Fig. 30

Cut and Paste

Type a few lines of text and highlight. Move the pointer onto the **Cut** button and click once and the text is deleted. Move the pointer to another part of the page and click once to move the text cursor into position. Now click on **Paste** and the line will be pasted into a new place.

Copy and Paste

Type a few lines of text. Highlight the first line. Move the pointer onto the button called **Copy** and click once. Now move the pointer so that it is at the end of the last word of the last line of text and click once. Notice that the text cursor on the screen is pulsing in the spot where you have just clicked. Move the pointer to the **Paste** function on the toolbar and click once. *Do not* click on the picture of the paintbrush. There should now be a copy of the first line that you highlighted at the end of your piece of text. This method can be used to highlight any part of the text and to copy it anywhere on the page or even to place it in another document.

Top Tip
It does take time to become proficient at the
function Cut, Copy and Paste, so keep
practising.

Section 16:
Copying Between Documents

Essential Information
One of the most useful aspects of Cut, Copy and Paste is
being able to copy from one document to another. It's in
this process that knowing how to minimise and restore a
page is essential. Refer back to Section 3 for how to Minimise
and Restore.

Action 1
Open up a new document (see Section 18) and type one
line of text. Now open up another new document and
type two lines of text. Highlight the two lines of text on
this second document and then click on the **Copy** button
on the toolbar.

Action 2
Minimise the second document.

Action 3
Place your cursor at the end of the line on the first document
and click once. Move the pointer onto the **Paste** button
on the toolbar and click once.

The lines from the second document will have been added to the line of the first document, thus combining the text of the two documents. In this way you can add sections of information from one document to another. You can also copy and paste between different programs. For example between Word and Excel or from a web page to Word.

Section 17:
The Menu Bar

At the top of the Word window is the **Menu Bar**. When the pointer is moved onto each word it becomes highlighted. By clicking on any one of these words, a drop down menu will be displayed. The words on each menu represent commands that operate the Word program.

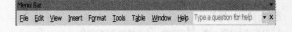

Fig. 31

Action 1

Place the pointer onto the word **File** and click once. The File drop-down menu is displayed.

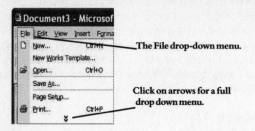

Fig. 32

Action 2
Click on each of the words on the menu bar and view the variety of tools that are available on each of the drop down menus. The following sections cover some of the functions on the File, Edit, View, Insert and Format menus.

Section 18:
Opening a New Document

Essential Information
Upon opening up the Microsoft Word program, a new clean page is displayed on the screen. Once this page has been utilised however, you will need to know how to open another new document.

Action 1
Move the pointer to the top of the screen and onto the menu bar and onto **File** and click once. A drop-down menu will appear.

Action 2

Move the pointer down the menu and the items will be highlighted in blue. Move the pointer onto **New** and click once with the left mouse button.

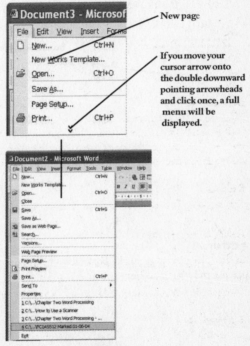

New page

If you move your cursor arrow onto the double downward pointing arrowheads and click once, a full menu will be displayed.

Fig. 33

Action 3

A box opens with a selection of both new and preformatted documents available.

Action 4

Click once on **Blank Document** to get a new page.

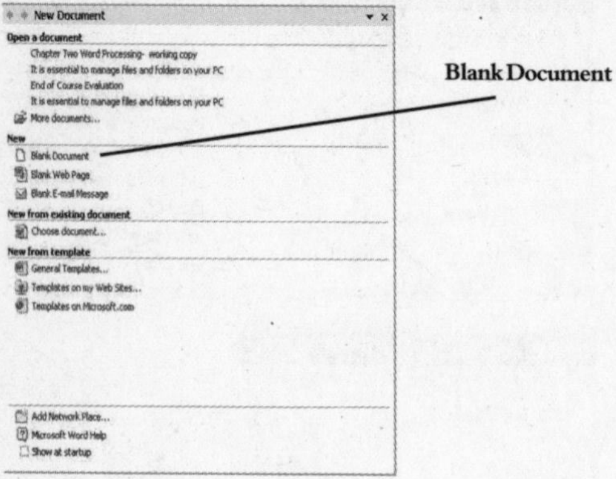

Fig. 34

Action 5

To close the new page, click once on the cross in the close box top right hand corner.

Section 19:
Saving a Document

Essential Information

Once you have created a document you will probably want to save it in order to work on it at a later date or to keep as a reference. It is possible to save a document onto various parts of the computer but it is easier to keep control if they are saved onto a floppy disk into the folder called **My Documents** which is on the computer's hard disk. (To save a document to a CD read *Chapter 5: How to Use Disks*.)

Action 1 (Saving onto My Documents)

Go to **File** on the menu bar and click once. The File drop-down menu appears. Move your pointer down the list until it highlights **Save As** click once.

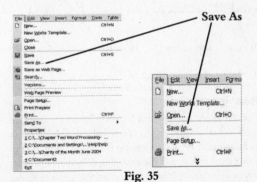

Fig. 35

Notice that in Figure 36 there are four white text boxes. The largest text box shows the names of documents that have previously been saved.

Save in   **Documents saved are listed in large text box**

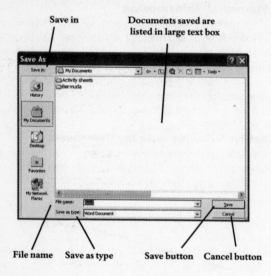

File name   Save as type   Save button   Cancel button

Fig. 36

Action 2

Each of the three narrow text boxes has a down arrow at one end. Click on the down arrow on the first text box called **Save in**. A drop down list is displayed showing the possible places to save a document (Fig. 37). It is important to look at this box before you save, as you need to know exactly where you are saving a document. The **My**

Document folder is held on the hard drive which is represented by HDD **(C:)** Move the pointer down the drop-down list, highlight HDD **(C:)** and click once (Fig. 37).

Action 3

Save in —

My Documents button —

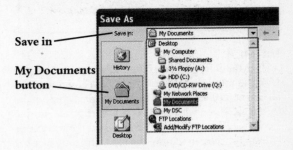

Fig. 37

Click on **My Documents**. My documents will be inserted into the **Save in** text box. The button on the left hand panel will also perform the same function. Click on the **My Documents** button and **My Documents** will appear in the **Save in** text box (Fig. 37).

Top Tip

To help keep your files organised, your document could be saved into a personal folder contained within My Documents. To know more about how to create and use folders, see *Chapter 7: How to create and manage files.*

Action 4

Look at the third text box called **File name**. This will show the name that the computer has chosen for your document. Usually this will be the very first words of the document. If you wish to select a different name for the document click once in the text box and the text cursor will appear. You can remove the name the computer has chosen and type in the new name for the document.

Action 5

The fourth text box is called **Save as type**. While you are working on word documents, select **Word Documents** (Fig. 36).

Action 6

Once you have typed the name that you have chosen for your document into the third text box, click on the **Save** button. Your document will now have been saved in **My Documents**. If you decide that you do not want to save yet, click on **Cancel**.

Top Tip

It's a good idea to practise saving a document. Don't worry if you can't remember it off by heart just yet, it takes a while to learn this procedure.

Section 20:
Saving to a floppy disk

Essential Information

If you do not know how to load a floppy disk, refer to Chapter 5, Section 2. Saving work onto a floppy disk involves almost the same procedure as saving into My Documents. The following actions will lead you through the process.

Action 1

Insert the floppy disk into the systems unit.

Action 2

Go to **File** on the menu bar and click once. The file drop-down menu appears. Move the pointer down the list until it highlights **Save As** and click once.

Action 3

Click on the down arrow on the first text box called **Save in** and a drop-down list appears. Click on **3½ Floppy** which will then be inserted into the text box.

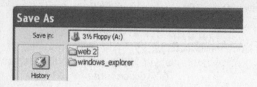

Fig. 38

Action 4

Look at the third text box called **File name** and remove the computer's selection by using Backspace or Delete and type in the new name for the document.

Action 5

In the fourth text box called **Save as type**, select **Word document**.

Action 6

Click on the **Save** button. Your document will now have been saved onto your floppy disk.

Top Tip

Do not remove the floppy disk while the red light is showing on the floppy disk drive or you may lose the material that you are saving.

Section 21:
Opening a Document from My Documents

Essential Information
Opening a document is a very similar operation to saving a document.

Action 1
Click on **File** on the menu bar and scroll down until you reach the word **Open.** Click once and the **Open** box is displayed.

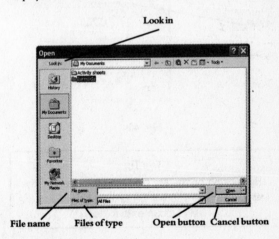

Fig. 39

Action 2

Click on the down arrow by the text box called **Files of Type** and make sure that **Word documents** or **All files** is selected.

Action 3

Click on the down arrow by the text box called **Look in**, and a drop-down list will appear. Click once on **My Documents** so that it is highlighted or click on the button **My Documents**.

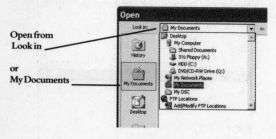

Open from
Look in

or
My Documents

Fig. 40

Top Tip

By clicking on the My Documents button on the left-hand panel you will be taken straight into the My Documents folder.

Action 4

Move the pointer onto the name of the document that you wish to open and click once, so that it is highlighted in blue. Click on **Open**. Your document will now appear on the screen.

Fig. 41

Section 22:
Opening a Document from Floppy Disk

Essential Information

Opening a document from a floppy disk is the same procedure as opening from My Documents. Just remember to insert the floppy disk into the floppy drive.

Action 1

Click on **File** on the menu bar and scroll down until you

reach the word **Open.** Click once and the open box will be displayed.

Action 2
In the **Look in** text box, click the down arrow and a drop-down list will appear.

Action 3
Move the pointer onto **3½ Floppy**, so that it is highlighted and click once.

Action 4
The large text box will now display the contents of the floppy disk.

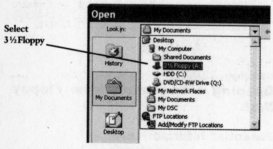

Select
3½ Floppy

Fig. 42

Action 5
Click on the arrow by the text box called **Files of type** and make sure that you select **Word Document** (or **All Files**).

Action 6

Move the pointer onto the name of the document that you wish to open and click once, so that it is highlighted in blue. Click on the word **Open**. The document will now appear on the screen.

Section 23:
Margins

Essential Information

Margins are set automatically by the computer. The top and bottom margins are set at 2.54 cm and the left and right margins are set at 3.17 cm. Because these sizes are set automatically by the computer they are known as the default sizes. On occasion, however, you may wish to alter the margins in order to contain the text in a smaller or larger area of the page.

Action 1

Open a new document. Go to **File** and click on **Page Setup**.

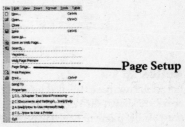

Page Setup

Fig. 43

Action 2

The **Page Setup** dialogue box is displayed (Fig. 44) . It has three tabs. Click once on the **Margins** tab.

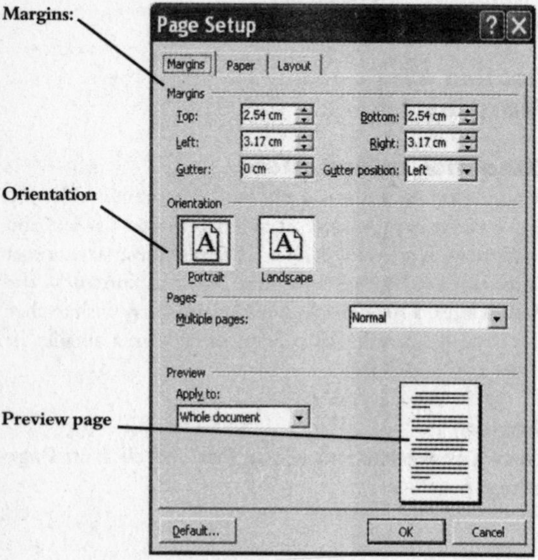

Margins: ──────

Orientation ──────

Preview page ──────

Page Setup	? X
Margins	Paper	Layout

Margins
Top: 2.54 cm   Bottom: 2.54 cm
Left: 3.17 cm   Right: 3.17 cm
Gutter: 0 cm   Gutter position: Left

Orientation
Portrait   Landscape

Pages
Multiple pages: Normal

Preview
Apply to:
Whole document

Default...   OK   Cancel

Fig. 44

Action 3

Locate the two boxes labelled **left** and **right.** Within these boxes are shown the sizes of the margins in centimetres (cm). At the moment they will probably show the default sizes.

By the side of the text boxes there are upward and downward pointing arrows. Use these to increase or decrease the size of the margins.

Action 4

Look at the **Preview** page on the right to see the effect of changing the numbers and therefore the size of the margins.

Action 5

When you want to keep the margins that you have set, click on **OK** and the new sizes will be applied to the page.

Action 6

The same technique can be used to alter the sizes of the top and bottom margins.

Section 24:
Print Preview

Essential Information

Print Preview allows a document to be viewed before time and paper is wasted in printing. It gives you the opportunity to discover any errors that may exist and to correct them before printing. It also enables you to see how well you have set out the text, so it is a good idea to get into the habit of previewing your work as you go along

Action 1

Open up a page of previously saved work or a blank page. Go to **File** on the menu bar and click once. Click once on **Print Preview** on the drop-down menu.

File	Edit	View	Insert	Format	Tools	Table

☐	New...	Ctrl+N
	New Works Template...	
🖿	Open...	Ctrl+O
	Close	
🖫	Save	Ctrl+S
	Save As...	
🖳	Save as Web Page...	
🖺	Search...	
	Versions...	
	Web Page Preview	
	Page Setup...	
🔍	Print Preview	
🖨	Print...	Ctrl+P
	Send To	▶
	Properties	
	1 C:\...\Chapter Two Word Processing- ...	
	2 C:\...\It is essential to manage file...	
	3 C:\...\End of Course Evaluation	
	4 C:\...\It is essential to manage file...	
	Exit	

Print preview → Print Preview

Fig. 45

Move the pointer onto the page on the screen and you will notice that the arrow becomes a magnifying glass. Click again and the page becomes enlarged; click once more and the page is returned to its previous size.

Action 2

Look at the print preview toolbar.

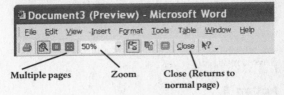

Multiple pages   Zoom   Close (Returns to
                                       normal page)

Fig. 46

On the screen, locate the buttons **Multiple Pages,
Zoom** and **Close**.

Action 3

Move the pointer to the **Multiple Pages** button and click
once. You now have a choice of how many pages to preview.

Move the pointer over the grid. You will notice that as
the pointer moves, pages on the grid are highlighted.
Highlight two pages on the grid and click once. Notice
that the single page has moved to the left to allow room for
a second page. In this way you can view up to six pages at
once.

Fig. 47

Action 4

The **Zoom** function allows you to increase and decrease the size of the page whilst in preview. Notice that the zoom function is showing a percentage size of the page while in preview.

Notice that to the right of the zoom button there is a down arrow.

Action 5

Click once on the down arrow and a drop-down list showing percentages is displayed.

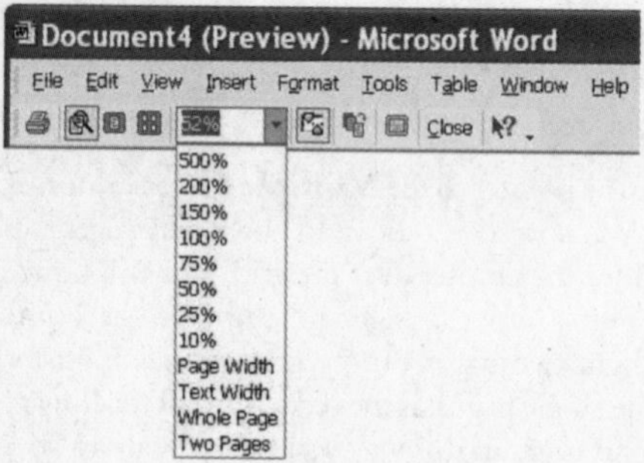

Fig. 48

Click on 10% and you will see that the page really does shrink. Now go back to the Zoom function and click on 50% and see how the page increases.

Action 6

Click on **Close** on the preview toolbar and you are returned to the normal page. You cannot make changes to the document whilst in Print Preview so if any need to be made you must always return to the normal page.

You should always save your document to preserve any changes that you have made.

Section 25:
Toolbars

Essential Information

Toolbars list utilities and functions for different programs. Open a new page in Word. Look at the top of the screen and as well as the menu bar there will probably be the Standard toolbar and the Formatting toolbar, all of which you have been using throughout this book. There may be other toolbars also visible: there are many that can be used for various purposes. It is very easy to mislay a toolbar, so don't panic if you lose one.

Action 1

To find the toolbars, go to **View** on the menu bar. Click once and highlight **Toolbars** on the drop-down menu. A list of different toolbars appears in another sub-menu. The ones that are currently displayed will have a tick by the side of them.

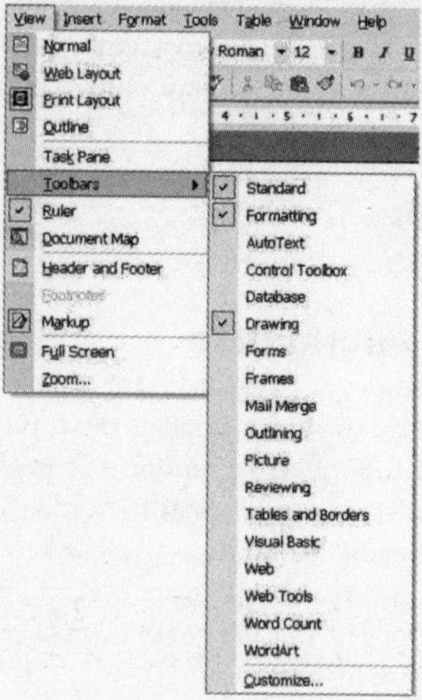

Fig. 49

Choose a toolbar that has not been ticked and click on it once. A new toolbar will appear on your screen.

Action 2

To remove the extra toolbar, go to **View** and click once. Select **Toolbars** and remove the tick by the toolbar that you wish to remove. Make sure that you retain the Standard and Formatting toolbars.

Top Tip

Remember, if you appear to have lost a
toolbar, go to View then Toolbars and make
sure that the relevant toolbar has a tick
against it.

Action 3

You can move toolbars around the screen. Look at the left-
hand side of the Standard and Formatting toolbars and the
Menu bar at the top of your page. On each grey strip there
appears to be a raised grey line. By placing your cursor on
these grey strips and using the method of click and drag it
is possible to move the toolbars and menu bars to other
areas of the screen which may be more convenient for you.

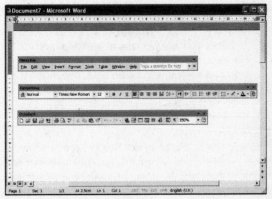

Fig. 50

Action 5

To replace the toolbars to the top of the screen, click once on the solid grey title bar and holding the button down, drag the bar back to the top of the screen. Wait until the bar becomes thinner and more elongated and then release the button.

Section 26:
Headers and Footers

Essential Information

The **Header** is the area of space at the very top of your page and the **Footer** is the area of space at the very bottom. Both Header and Footer give you the opportunity to utilise the whole page.

Top Tip

When you are working in Headers and Footers, the text on the main document will fade and so you will not be able to work on it until you close the Header and Footer toolbar.

The title can be placed in the Header section while the Footer section provides space to insert footnotes or page numbers. Anything you wish can be placed in these spaces: logos, graphics, dates and even pictures.

Action 1

Go to **View** on the menu bar and click on **Header and Footer**.

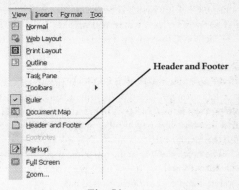

Fig. 51

Action 2

A new toolbar called **Header and Footer** appears on the screen (Fig. 52).

If you allow the pointer to rest on each symbol, the name of the function will appear on the screen. Identify the various symbols on the toolbar.

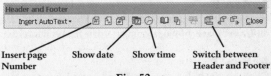

Insert page Number | Show date | Show time | Switch between Header and Footer

Fig. 52

Action 3

Click on **Switch between Header and Footer**. This allows you to switch between the top of the page and the bottom. Click on Switch between Header and Footer again and you will be back where you started.

Click on **Close** on the Header and Footer Toolbar.

Action 4

Open up a document that you have previously saved. If you have not yet saved a document, then create one by typing a few lines. Click on **View**, and then click on **Header and Footer**. The new toolbar appears on the screen and also the header.

The header will be at the top of the page and will appear as a dotted line box. It will have the word **Header** in the top left-hand corner of the dotted box.

Action 5

Notice how the writing of your document has faded; this reminds you that while you are working in Header and Footer you will not be able to write on the main document. The text cursor is already blinking in the header and is thus ready for you to type. Type in a title for the document.

Action 6

Now go to the **Header and Footer** toolbar and click once on **Insert Date**. Notice that today's date has been inserted.

Action 7

Click on **Switch between Header and Footer**. You

should now be looking at the footer. If not, click again on **Switch between Header and Footer**.

Action 8

Now click on **Insert page number**. Notice that a number has been added to the bottom of the page. Now click on **Insert Time**. Notice that the time has also been added to the footer.

Action 9

Click on **Close** on the Header and Footer toolbar. You will now be returned to the main body of your document. Save your document.

Action 10

If you want to view the changes that you have made to your document, click on **File** then **Print Preview** and view it there. (See Section 24.)

Section 27:
Viewing the Page

Essential Information

There are various options available to view the Word page. These can be found on the **View** drop-down menu and in the bottom left-hand corner of the window. The options are Normal, Web Layout, Print Layout and Outline. The simplest to use are Normal and Print Layout. Normal carries a horizontal ruler at the top of the page and Print Layout a horizontal and vertical ruler.

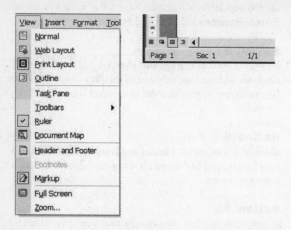

Fig. 53

Top Tip
If the appearance of your page suddenly
changes, it may that you have accidentally
clicked on one of the page layout buttons,
situated in the bottom left-hand corner of the
window. Try clicking on each of the buttons in
turn, to return your page to its previous
appearance.

Section 28:
The Ruler

Essential Information

The presence of the ruler is helpful in organising the layout of your page. It is possible to customise the page so that the ruler is either visible or hidden.

Action 1

Click on **View** on the menu bar and on the drop-down list find **Ruler** (Fig. 53). To make it visible, click on **Ruler** so that a tick appears next to it. If you are in Normal view the ruler at the top of the page will be visible. If you are in Print Layout view both the horizontal and vertical ruler will be visible. To hide the Ruler, click on **Ruler** on the **View** drop-down menu, and remove the tick.

Section 29:
Line Spacing

Essential Information

So far all your typing has probably been in single line spacing. It is possible, however, to automatically type text in other sizes of spacing.

Action 1

Go to **Format** and click once. Click on **Paragraph.**

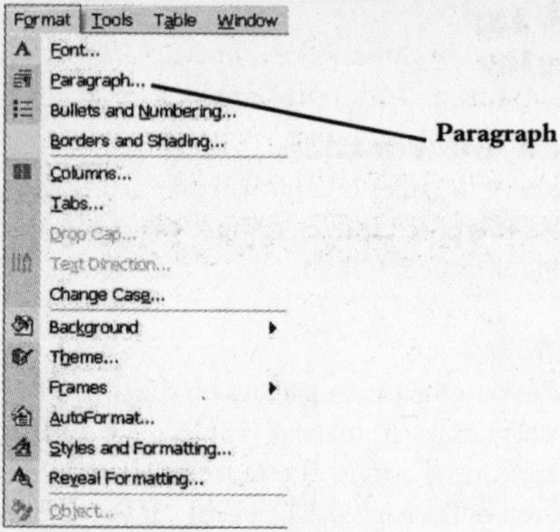

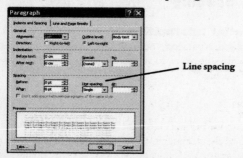

Fig. 54

Action 2

A box appears called **Paragraph** (Fig . 55). It has two tabs at the top. Choose **Indents and Spacing**.

Fig. 55

Action 3

The box contains a number of text boxes. One of them is
called **Line spacing.** Within this text box will be written
Single. At the side of the box is a triangle (down arrow).
Click on it and a drop down list is displayed.

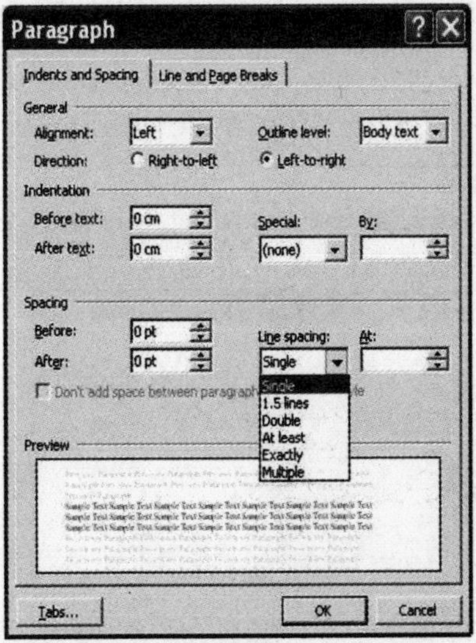

Fig. 56

Action 4

Highlight **Double** and click once. Click **OK** and you are
returned to the document. Now type a few lines of text
using the Wraparound function: *do not* press Enter. Because

you have already chosen double spacing, your text should automatically be double-spaced.

Action 5

Highlight the document that you have just typed in double spacing. Click on **Format** and then click on **Paragraph**. Find the **Line spacing** box and this time select Single spacing and click **OK**. You are returned to your document and the text is now in single line spacing.

Action 6

The **Paragraph** box also allows you to change the alignment of your text.

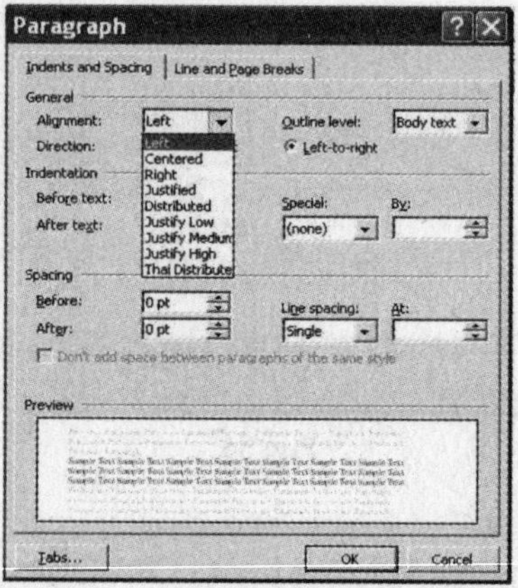

Fig. 57

Look at the top left-hand side of the box and find the title called **Alignment**. Click on the down arrow and a drop-down list appears. Here you will see the words, **Left, Centered, Right** and **Justified**. These perform the same functions as the alignment buttons on the Formatting toolbar. Going through **Paragraph** is just another way of reaching this function, and if you are changing your line spacing it may be quicker for you to select the alignment of your document at the same time.

Section 30:
Bullets and Numbering

Essential Information

It is possible to select various styles of numbering and bullets to suit different documents. Once your selection has been made it is then possible to include the bullets and numbering on your page by using the appropriate button on the toolbar. This allows you to decide where and when to use a bullet or a number. Microsoft Word will automatically insert a number or bullet every time you press Enter. When you want to stop using this function, press Enter twice or deactivate by clicking on the relevant button on the Formatting toolbar. First you need to select a style of bullets or numbers, so follow the steps below.

Action 1

Click on **Format** on the menu bar. A drop-down menu appears. Click on **Bullets and Numbering.**

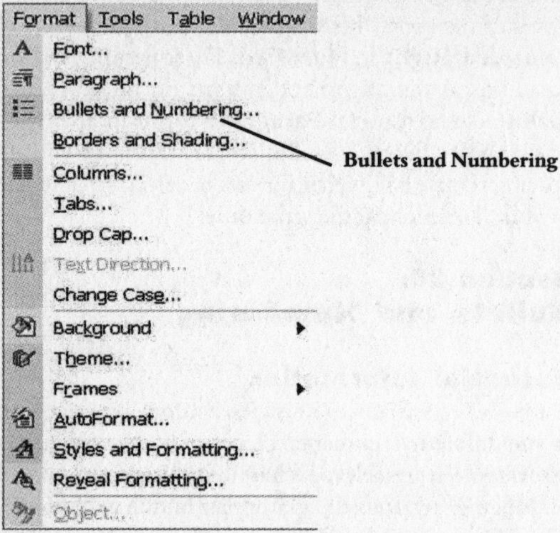

Fig. 58

Action 2

Notice that the **Bullets and Numbering** dialogue box that appears on the screen has four different tabs (Fig. 59). They are Bulleted, Numbered, Outline Numbered and List styles.

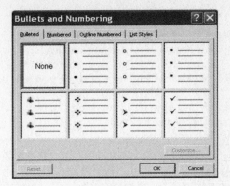

Fig. 59

Click on the tab called **Bulleted**. As you can see from Figure 59, seven different styles of bullets are shown on the Bulleted tab. At the moment the box **None** is highlighted by a thick blue border. This shows that at the moment no style of bullet has been selected.

Action 3
Choose a style that you prefer by clicking on it and then click **OK** at the bottom of the box. Your page is now ready for automatic bullets. As you type and press Enter a bullet will appear on the page.

Action 4
To select **Numbered** go to Format, select Bullets and Numbering and the tab called **Numbered**. Seven style

options appear. Click on any style.

Action 5

Look at the bottom of the box and identify the following:

Restart numbering   **Continue previous list**

Make sure that **Restart numbering** (Fig. 60) has been selected: click on the circle and a black dot will appear in the centre, indicating selection.

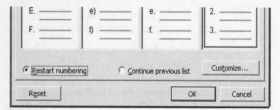

Fig. 60

Click on **OK** and the box disappears and your page is ready for typing. Notice that the numbering button on the menu bar is now depressed. (If you wish to stop this function simply click once on the relevant button on the toolbar.) Your page is now ready for typing with automatic numbering. Whenever you press Enter a number will be placed on the page. To remove any unwanted numbers that may appear, or if you make a mistake, position the cursor in the correct place and then press backspace to delete.

Action 6

On the Formatting toolbar are the two buttons that allow you to use bullets and numbers whenever and wherever you wish (Fig. 61).

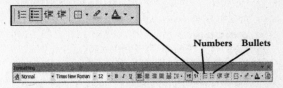

Numbers   Bullets

Fig. 61

Once you have selected a type of bullet or number, these buttons can be used to switch the function on and off as and when needed.

Section 31:
Find and Replace

Essential Information

Find and replace enables you to save time in replacing one word within your text with a different one. It is useful if you have repeatedly misspelt a word or need to find a particular word in a long document in order to change it for another.

Action 1

Click on **Edit**. On the drop-down menu that appears click on **Find**.

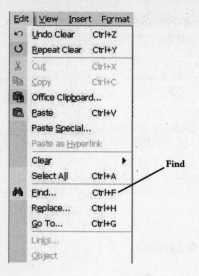

Find

Fig. 62

Action 2

The **Find and Replace** box is displayed. Notice that it has three tabs at the top: **Find, Replace** and **Go To.** Click on **Replace (Fig. 63)**.

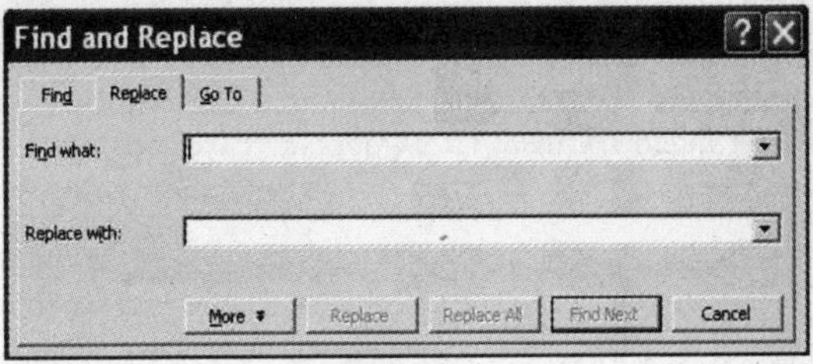

Fig. 63

Action 3

In the **Find what:** text box type in the word that you wish to be removed and in the **Replace with:** text box, type in the replacement word. The program searches and highlights each instance of the word. Click on the **Replace** button to replace.

Action 4

If you do not wish to go through all the text looking at each word individually, you can replace all the examples of the unwanted word by clicking on **Replace all**.

Section 32:
Insert Symbols

You may at some point need a symbol that is not present on the keyboard e.g. scientific notation or fractions.

Action 1

Place your text cursor within the text where the symbol is to go. Click on **Insert** on the menu bar and click on

Symbol on the drop-down menu. The Symbol window opens (Fig. 64). From here you can select from a variety of symbols. Click on the symbol required and then click on **Insert** and then **Close**. The symbol will have been inserted into the text.

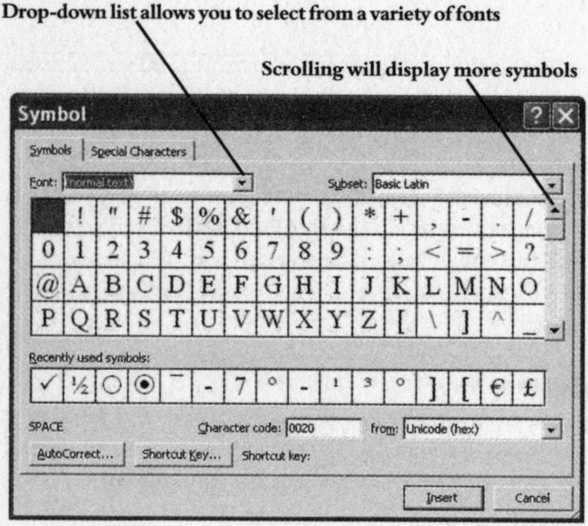

Drop-down list allows you to select from a variety of fonts

Scrolling will display more symbols

Fig. 64

Section 33:
Inserting a Picture

Action 1

Go to **Insert** on the menu bar. Move the cursor onto

Picture on the drop-down menu. A sub-menu appears.
This sub menu allows you access to the pictures stored on
your hard disk or on CD. Click on **Clip Collection** to
view the pictures provided by Microsoft (you may need to
insert a CD) or click on **From File** to view pictures that
you have saved.

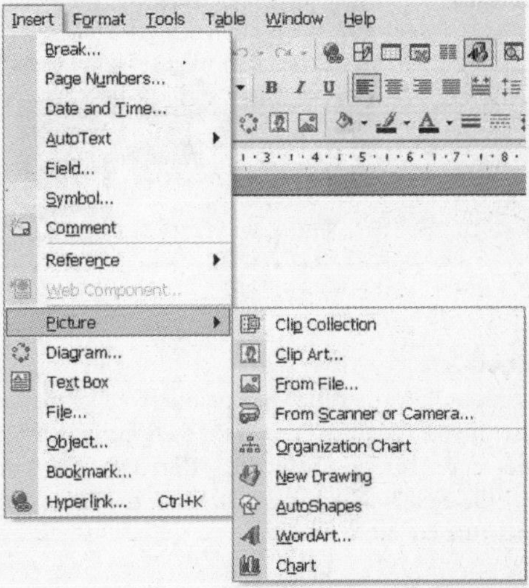

Fig. 65

An **Insert** window will appear (Fig. 66). Click on the picture
you require and then click on **Insert** (for Clip Collection
also click on **Close**). The picture will be inserted into your
Word document.

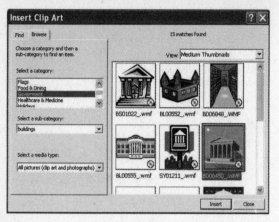

Fig. 66

Action 2

Experiment in formatting your picture by clicking on the picture in your document, and then clicking on **Format** on the menu bar, and selecting **Picture**. The Format Picture dialogue box allows you to resize the picture and to organise the layout.

Section 34:
Shortcuts

Look at the first three pictures on the Standard toolbar. Then look at the drop-down menu from File on the menu bar. These pictures are repeated, along with the name of the function.

Fig. 67: Standard Toolbar

Shortcut to New

Look for the word **New** and the small picture of a new page on the **File** drop-down menu. Look on the Standard toolbar and find the same picture. This is the shortcut. Click once to open a new page.

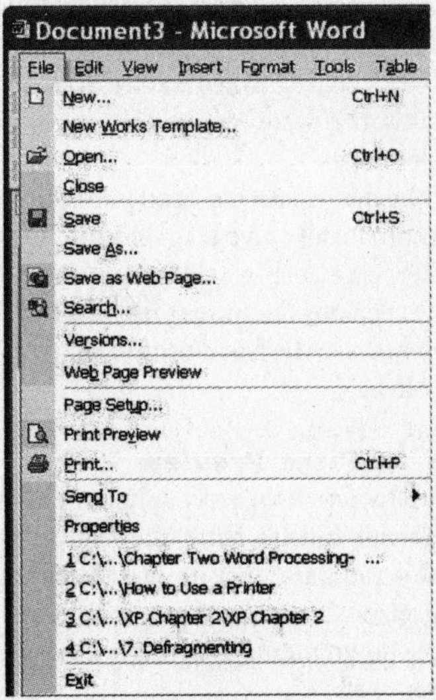

Fig. 68

Shortcut to Open

Look on the **File** drop-down menu and find the word **Open**. Look on the Standard toolbar and find the same picture of the open yellow folder. Click once on the folder and the normal Open box appears on the screen.

Shortcut to Save

Look at the File drop-down menu and find the word **Save**. Locate the picture of a Floppy disk on the Standard toolbar. This is the shortcut to saving a document. There are two points to remember about this shortcut:

1. If it is the first time that the document has been saved, the **Save As** box will appear on the screen as normal.
2. If the document has been previously saved it will automatically save it again into the same place. The **Save As** box will not appear. So if you wish to save your document into a different location, do not use the **Save** button on the Standard toolbar.

Shortcut to Print Preview

The Standard toolbar also carries a shortcut to Print Preview. It is the seventh button from the left on the Standard toolbar and is the same picture of a sheet of paper and a magnifying glass shown by the words Print Preview on the File drop-down menu. Use this button as a shortcut to preview your work.

Shortcut to Print

The sixth button from the left on the Standard toolbar is a shortcut to Print. However this does not provide you with the opportunity to select a page range or number of copies. To do this you must go to the File drop-down menu.

Shortcuts to Recent Documents

There are two other quick ways of opening a recent file. If you are already in Word, click on **File** and at the bottom of the drop-down menu you will see a list of the most recently opened documents. Single-click on the name of the document to open it.

Another quick route is through the Start menu. Click once on **Start** and move the pointer onto **My Recent Documents**. A list of recently opened files will appear. Click on the file you wish to open.

Section 35:
Word Templates and Wizards

Essential Information

Word Templates and Wizards are preformatted sample documents that take the hard work out of deciding how to set out a particular type of document. The Wizard leads you through various stages to complete the template. The **Memo** and **Envelope Wizard** for example, will help you create correctly formatted and well laid out memos and envelopes. There are many different types of templates available. All you have to do is replace the sample text with your text. There are an extensive range of templates.

Action 1

Click on **File** on the menu bar and then click on **New** and then on **General Templates** from the new window that opens (Fig. 69).

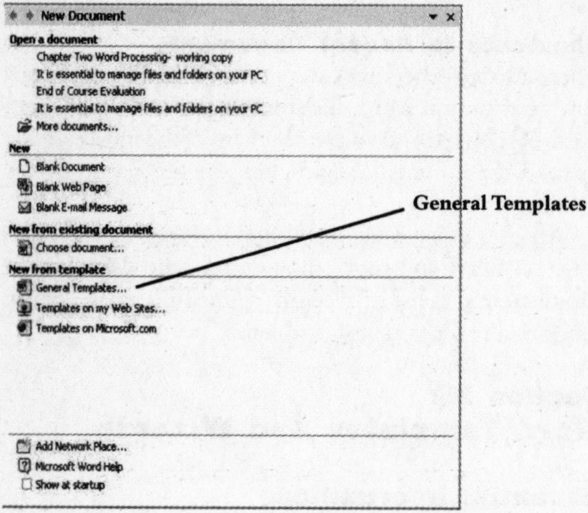

Fig. 69

Action 2

A box will open displaying a number of tabs with different headings. Click on each of the tabs to view the variety of templates available.

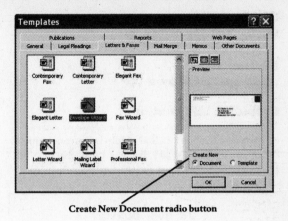

Create New Document radio button

Fig. 70

Action 3

When you have found a template that suits your purpose, simply click on the icon, make sure that the radio button called **Create New Document** is activated and then click **OK.** The Word wizard will lead you through the process. That's all there is to it!

Chapter Three:
How to Use Help

Section 1:
Help on Windows XP

Essential Information

The Help system is comprehensive, easy to use and can be context sensitive. You will find a **Help** button on the menu bar of most windows and dialogue boxes that you use. Help can also be found on the Start menu.

Jargon Buster
Context sensitive

Relating directly to the operation being carried out.

Section 2
Finding the Help and Support
Center

Essential Information

The Help and Support Center can be found on the **Start** menu and by clicking on the **Help** menu on an open window.

Action 1

Go to the **Start** menu and click on **Help and Support**.

How to use Help

Fig. 1

Action 2

If you already have a window open, click on **Help** on the menu bar, and then click on **Help and Support Center**.

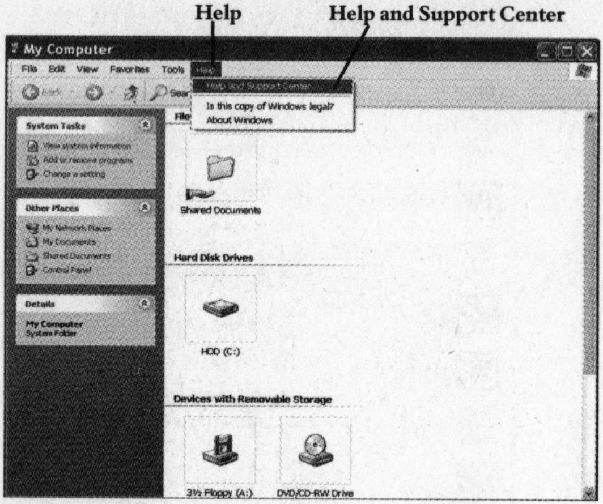

Help   Help and Support Center

Fig. 2

Section 3:
Using the Help and Support Center

Essential Information

The Help and Support Center on your PC will look similar
to the picture below. There may be minor differences, due
to it being modified by the supplier of your PC or whether
you have a home or professional edition of Windows XP.
There are various ways in which you can use the Help and
Support Center to search for information and assistance.

You can pick a topic, a task or search for a specific item in the search box. The following is an example of using Help for information about printing.

Action 1

Under the list of topics, click on **Printing and Faxing**.

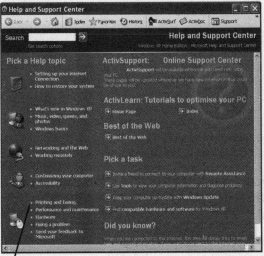

Fig. 3

Click on Printing and Faxing

Action 2

Click on Printing.

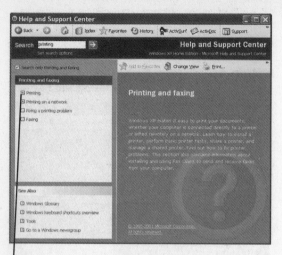

Fig. 4

Click on Printing

Action 3

A sub menu opens on the left, listing further topics. Click on the topic that meets your requirements and a further list opens on the right pane of the window. Click on the one that interests you.

Click on Basic Printing Tasks and a further list opens on the right.

Click on Print a document

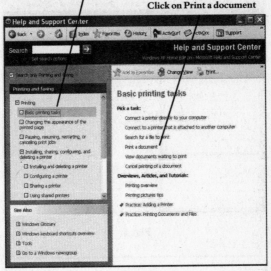

Fig. 5

Action 4

The information about that task is then displayed on the right pane of the window.

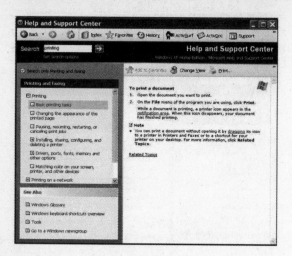

Fig. 6

Top Tip

Using Help is an excellent way of extending your knowledge and increasing your confidence. Look on it as a built-in manual that will enable you to discover more about your PC programs.

Section 4:
Help and Support Center Search Box

Essential Information
Sometimes it is quicker to use the search box to find the information that you require.

Action 1
Type into the search box the name of the item which interests you and then click on the green arrow to the right of the search box.

Action 2
A list of results will be displayed on the left pane of the window. Click on a topic and details are displayed in the right pane.

Type in the search box   Click on the green arrow

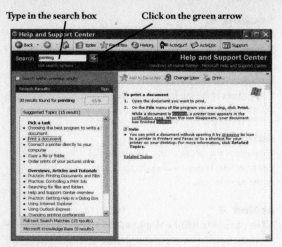

Fig. 7

Click on Print a document and the information is shown on the right pane.

Section 5:
What's This? On Dialogue Boxes

Essential Information

What's This? is a very useful tool, especially for beginners. It acts as a reminder of various functions and features. It is also known as context sensitive help.

**Dialogue box question mark
in top right-hand corner**

'Point and tell'

It can be found by clicking on the question mark in the top right-hand corner of a dialogue box. The pointer then changes to a cursor with a question mark attached. This is called a 'point and tell' system. Follow the example below to see how **What's This ?** works.

Action 1

Go to the Start menu and click on Control Panel. Click on Printers and Other Hardware. Double-click on the Mouse icon and open **Mouse Properties** (Fig. 8). Click on the question mark in the top right –hand corner,

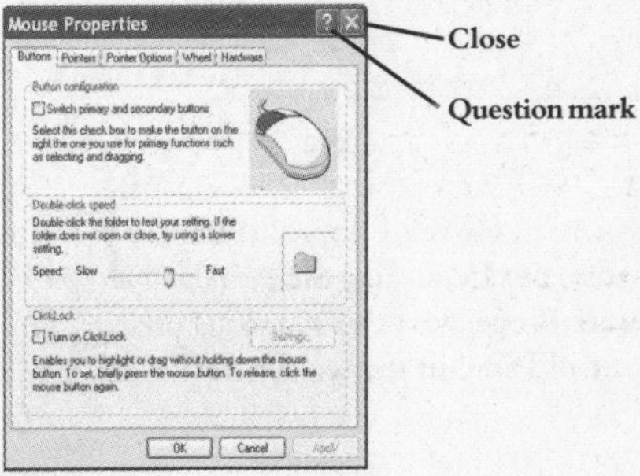

Fig. 8

Action 2

Move the cursor (now in the shape of a question mark and arrow) across the screen and onto the yellow folder, click once and a yellow explanation box will appear.

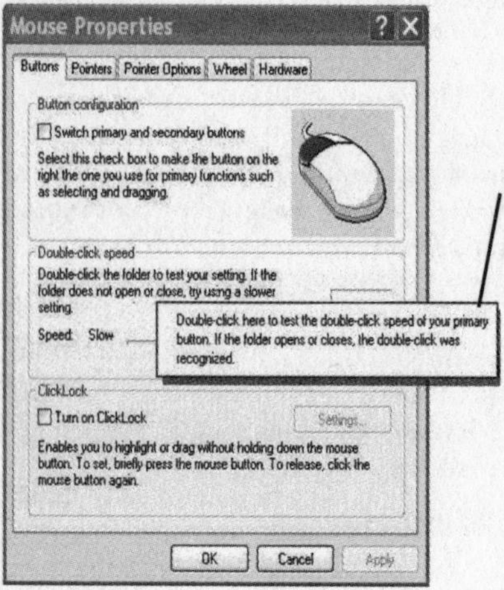

Fig. 9

After you have read the explanation, remove the explanation box by clicking once on the dialogue box. Close the Mouse Properties box by clicking on the Close box and the Control Panel in the same way.

Section 6:
What's This? On Microsoft Word

Action 1

Open Microsoft Word. Click on **Help** on the menu bar, and select **What's This?** from the drop-down menu.

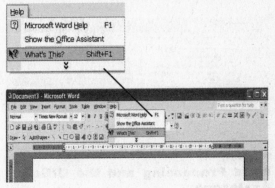

Fig. 10

Action 2

Move the cursor, now in the shape of an arrow and a question mark, across the screen and click once on the **Bold** button. A yellow box pops up with an explanation of the **Bold** function. Read the explanation and then remove it by clicking on the yellow box.

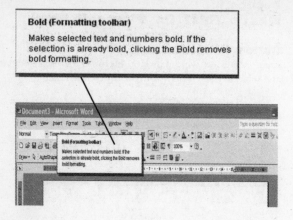

Fig. 11

Section 7:
Word Processing and the Office Assistant

Essential Information

The Office Assistant enables you to ask a direct question and helps you to solve word processing problems. It can be called up by clicking on the question mark on the Standard toolbar.

Fig. 12

Action 1

Open the Office Assistant and a text box will be displayed. Delete the words 'Type your question here and then click Search' and type in your own question.

Fig. 13

Click once on **Search** and the results will be displayed.

In Figure 14 the Office Assistant shows the first five results to a query on how to print. By clicking on **See more**, another five results are listed as in Figure 15.

To return to previous answers, click on See previous.

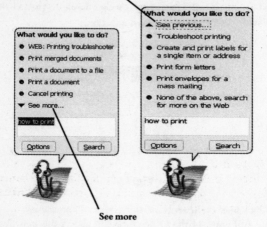

See more

Fig. 14   Fig. 15

Action 2

To view a search result, double click on a relevant item.

Section 8:
Show or Hide the Office Assistant

It is possible to hide the Office Assistant, so that it only appears at your invitation. It can be recalled at your command by following Action 2.

Action 1

To hide the Office Assistant, click on the **Help** button on the menu bar, and from the drop-down menu, select **Hide the Office Assistant**.

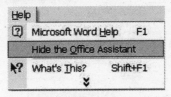

Fig. 16

Action 2

To show the Office Assistant, return to the **Help** button and on the drop-down menu, click on **Show Office Assistant**.

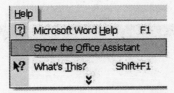

Fig. 17

Section 9:
Changing the Office Assistant

There are a variety of Office Assistants to choose from. The one below is called Clippit but it is very easy to select another.

Action 1

Call up the Office Assistant by clicking on the question mark on the toolbar. Then place your cursor on top of Clippit – *not* on the text box – and right click. A drop-down menu appears.

Fig. 18

Action 2

Click on **Choose Assistant** and the **Office Assistant Gallery** is displayed.

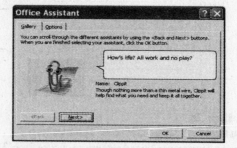

Fig. 19

As you click on **Next>**, various office assistants will be previewed. When you find one that you like, click on **OK** and your new selection will replace Clippit.

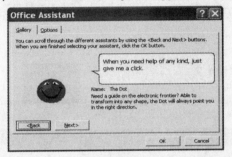

Fig. 20: The Dot – an alternative to Clippit

Section 10:
Microsoft Word Help

Essential Information
Microsoft Word Help is another useful tool and can be found in the top right-hand corner of the Word window.

Action 1
Click in the text box **Type a question for help** and type in the name of the topic. Here, in Figure 21, we typed in 'printing' and then pressed **Enter** on the keyboard.

Fig. 21

Action 2

A drop down list is displayed allowing a topic to be selected. In Figure 22, we double clicked on **Print a document to a file**.

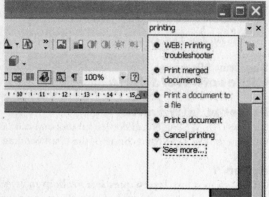

Fig. 22

Action 3

Microsoft Word Help is displayed (Fig. 23). On the right

pane is the information about printing a document to a file. On the left pane is a list of the contents of Word Help. To view further topics simply click on a folder to open.

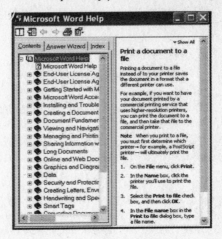

Fig. 23

Section 11:
Microsoft Works Help

Action 1

Open Microsoft Works Task Launcher and click on **Help** .

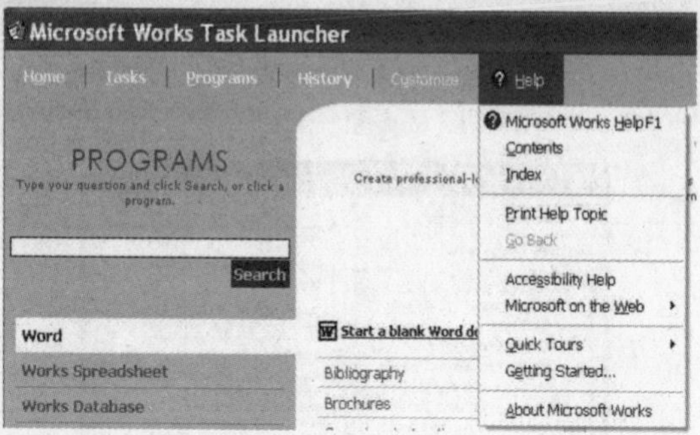

Fig. 24

A drop-down menu is displayed. Click on **Microsoft Help F1**.

Action 2

Works Help opens (Fig. 25). Type your query in the text box and then click on the **Search** button. The results of your search will be displayed in the pane below the text box.

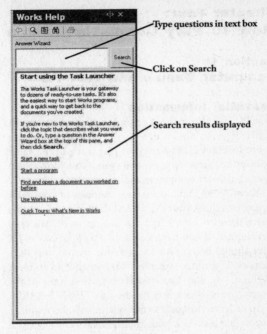

Fig. 25

Section 12:
Microsoft Help on the Web

Additional help can be found by connecting directly to Microsoft via the Internet. To do this click on **Help** on the menu bar, select **Office on the Web** and follow the instructions given.

Chapter Four:
How to Play Computer Games

Section 1:
Computer Games and Your PC

Essential Information

Your PC will already hold a number of computer games from Microsoft. These can be easily played and are simple to use (Section 2). However, to play some of the more sophisticated games you need to ensure that your system has the necessary equipment and accessories.

Some games take up a large amount of computer memory so check your PC's RAM. Broadly speaking, the newer the game, the larger the amount of PC memory they require. If you have a computer with Windows XP, there should be no problem with the size of your PC's memory. If you have installed Windows XP on an older machine, you may have problems playing some of the newest games, which may require up to 256 MB RAM.

In order to run games your system will also require a suitable graphics card. Initially the graphics card already in your PC will be adequate. However, as you gain in expertise and experience you may wish to upgrade to a new graphics card with its own processor. This will have the effect of making the games more realistic and faster.

If you are unsure about any of these aspects, contact your retailer or a computer engineer to advise you.

There are three different types of computer games: the standard Microsoft games already loaded onto your PC, games on CD or DVD and games on the Internet.

Section 2: Standard Microsoft Games

Essential Information

There are a number of games on the Microsoft menu: Solitaire, FreeCell, Minesweeper, Hearts, Spider Solitaire, Pinball and some that you need to connect to the Internet to play. They form a good introduction to how some of the less complex games are played. To access any of these games, click on the **Start** button on the Taskbar, **All Programs** and then **Games**.

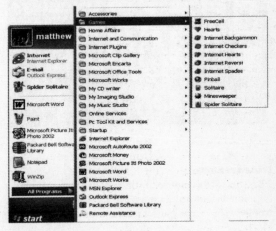

Fig. 1

Solitaire

To play Solitaire see Chapter One, Section 6.

FreeCell

The object of this game is to move all four suits in their correct numerical order into the spaces in the top right corner (Fig. 2). Click on **Help** on the FreeCell menu bar for more on how to play this game.

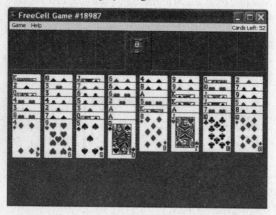

Fig. 2

Minesweeper

The object of this game is to achieve the maximum number of points before being blown up! Click on **Help** on the Minesweeper menu bar for more information on how to play.

Fig. 3

Hearts

When you play Hearts you will firstly be asked, as the fourth player, to enter your name. When you have done so, click **OK** and the game will open (Fig. 4). The object is to lose all your cards by scoring the lowest number of points. For more on how to play, click on **Help** on the Hearts menu.

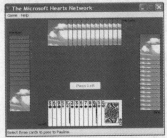

Fig. 4

3D Pinball

The aim of 3D Pinball is to launch the ball, and then earn as many points as possible by hitting bumpers, targets and flags (Fig. 5). The game is divided into nine levels of play, the higher the level, the more difficult it is to earn points. For more on how to play, click on Help on the Pinball menu.

Fig. 5

Spider Solitaire

The purpose of Spider Solitaire is to remove all the cards from the packs at the top of the page, in the fewest number of moves. There are three levels of difficulty (Fig. 6). You can play using just one pack of cards or increase the difficulty and play with two or four packs. When you have selected a level, the game opens (Fig. 7). For more on how to play, click on **Help** on the Spider Solitaire menu bar.

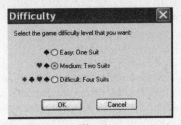

Fig. 6

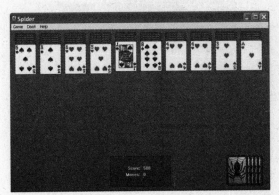

Fig. 7

Jargon Buster
Freebies
Free software available to download from the Internet.

Microsoft Internet Games

On the Games menu is a selection of games which can only be accessed through the Internet. They are Backgammon, Checkers, Hearts, Reversi and Spades. When you click any of them you will be asked to connect to the internet (Fig. 8). If you decide to proceed, remember that you are using a phone line and therefore paying for playing.

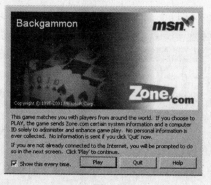

Fig. 8

Section 3:
Games on CD or DVD

Essential Information

An enormous number of games of varying degrees of complexity are available on CD and DVD. They range from traditional board games to the very latest 3D video-like adventures.

These can be as diverse as anything produced by the film industry: from spy thrillers and mystery and sci-fi and fantasy.

You can role-play by visiting historical battle scenes, drive a steam train, or save the world from aliens!

Games are controlled on the screen by the mouse or, if you prefer, you can use joysticks, gamepads or steering wheels. These are accessories which can be obtained from any computer or department store.

They are plugged into the game port of the systems unit and provide precision control and the use of action buttons. They also come with a CD-ROM which tells the computer that you have attached a new piece of hardware.

Action 1

Ensure your system has enough memory. Always check the games packaging for the size of memory required in order to avoid overloading the system.

Action 2

Connect your joystick, gamepad or steering wheel to the game port and make sure that you have run the accompanying CD-ROM, so that the computer is aware of the new hardware.

Action 3

Load the game CD or DVD into the correct tray in the usual way and then follow the instructions. If you have problems in running the CD or DVD, refer to *Chapter 5: How to Use Disks, Play Music and Watch Movies.*

Top Tip

Be sociable! Instead of the computer being the opponent, use a pair of gamepads or joysticks to compete against friends and family.

Section 4:
Games on the Internet and Game Developers

Many games can be downloaded from the Internet and most game developers also have their own web sites that give previews and information about the games that they have on offer. It is possible to obtain some for free and others are available on a trial basis. Then if you don't like it, you don't have to buy it.

There are three ways of playing online: against the computer, against another player, or against a group of players. Companies such as Microsoft and Virgin run game sites where you can link up with others to play your chosen game. Game sites are opening up and closing down all the time, so the best way to find what is around at any point in time is to ask a search engine for the latest sites. Ask Jeeves, for example, produced a list of sites in the UK and elsewhere, some with free downloads (Fig. 9).

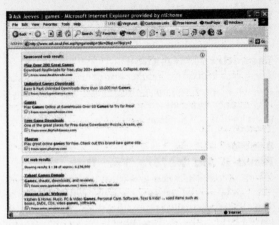

Fig. 9

Jargon Buster
Cheats

These are articles, magazines and books written about how to play certain games and the best way to win. They detail shortcuts to becoming more proficient at games currently on the market. Many game sites on the Internet also have a section called 'Cheats'. Look out for them when you pay the site a visit.

Section 5:
Games Magazines

Essential Information

There are a variety of computer magazines available today and many have details on playing games on the computer. It's probably a good idea to browse through some of them to get an idea of what is on offer.

Section 6:
Have a Go Before You Buy

If you are completely new (a newbie) to computer games, then a good way of getting an introduction to them is to visit a large department or computer store where there will usually be systems already set up with games for you to try out. You can also test a variety of accessories such as joy sticks and steering wheels, and get some idea of how they work and which one is for you.

Chapter Five:
How to Use Disks, Play Music and Watch Movies

Section 1:
Types of Disks

Essential information
There are three types of disk that you can use on your computer. They are:

3½" Floppy

CD

DVD

3½" Floppy
The standard 3½" floppy disk has a rigid plastic body which contains a thin flexible magnetic disk. At one end is a slider which protects the disk from dust and damage. When the disk is placed into the computer's floppy disk slot, the slider moves across to allow the machine to read or write onto the magnetic disk.

Floppy disks are a quick, cheap and easy way of storing information from your computer and for transporting information from one computer to another. However, they hold a limited amount of information and eventually become full.

Compact Disks

There are two types:

CD-ROM

If you already use a CD player then you will probably be aware that that a CD-ROM is a silver-coloured plastic disc that can store an amazing amount of information. But besides carrying music, a CD can also hold a computer program, a computer game, an encyclopaedia, a supermarket shopping trolley and a whole variety of other things – the list is virtually endless.

CD-R and CD-RW

These are used for saving your work and storing information. They are more expensive than floppy disks but hold much more data.

Digital Disk – otherwise known as DVD

A DVD is similar to a CD in appearance. If you have a newer system, then you will probably have a separate DVD drawer. It is now possible to use DVD to play films on your computer.

Jargon Buster

CD-ROM stands for **C**ompact **D**isk – **R**ead **O**nly **M**emory. This means that you can only read information from the disk and are unable to use it for saving your own information.

CD-R stands for **C**ompact **D**isk – **R**ecordable.

CD-RW stands for **C**ompact **D**isk – **ReW**ritable

DVD stands for **D**igital **V**ersatile **D**isk

Section 2:
How to load and eject a 3 ½" Floppy

Action 1
Identify the Floppy disk slot in your systems unit. Insert the floppy, slider first. If it does not easily go into the slot, turn it over and try the other way around.

Action 2
To eject the floppy, press the button adjacent to the disk.

Action 3
To discover how to save and open files and folders on a floppy disk, see Chapter 2.

Section 3:
How to Insert, Eject and Autorun a CD-ROM or DVD

Top Tip

Hold a CD-ROM or DVD disk by the edges and never on the face on the disk. Dirt and finger marks can seriously damage the surface.

Action 1

Top Tip

Can I use a CD or a DVD in any drawer? No! Use the drawers allocated for each disk. If you do get them mixed up and place a disk in the wrong drawer, don't panic. It will simply not run, as it will not be compatible with the reader. If you have a PC with one drawer for both CD and DVD this problem will naturally not arise.

Switch on your computer and wait until your Windows application has finished loading. On the front of your systems unit should be one or perhaps two retractable trays (or drives), which hold the disks. Identify the correct drive. If you have two, one will be for a CD and the other a DVD. Press the button on the front of the drive and wait until the drawer opens out towards you. If you have just one tray, then it will be a combined drive for both CD and DVD.

Action 2

Place the disk in the drawer with the label upwards. Gently push the drawer back into the computer. To eject the disk, press the button adjacent to the drawer.

Action 3

Many disks will now Autorun and you will begin to see the program being loaded onto the screen. Should the disk fail to Autorun, look in the disk case for information and follow the instructions included. If it still does not run, go to Section 4.

A DVD should run automatically but if you are having problems phone the helpline on the disk packaging. (Check how much they charge per minute before you call.)

Section 4:
CD-ROM that does not Autorun

Action 1

Click once on **Start,** then click on **Run** and a dialogue box called **Run** opens (Fig. 1). Sometimes just clicking on Run alerts the computer that there is a disk in the drive and it will then Autorun. If not, go to Action 2.

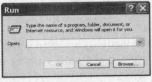

Fig. 1

Action 2

Click in the text box of the Run dialogue box and try typing one of the following, then click OK. (Q is the letter of your CD drive.)

> Q:\START.EXE
> Q:\AUTORUN.EXE
> Q:\SETUP
> Q:\ *name of program*   \START.EXE
> Q:\ *name of program*   \SETUP.EXE

In the last two instances, type in the name of the program that you are installing. If none of the above has worked, try typing the same phrases (one at a time) but this time in lower case.

Top Tip

To check the drive that is used for your DVD/CD, click on Start, then on **My Computer**. A window will open and you will see the following icon:

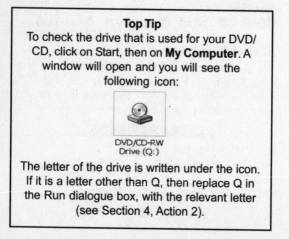

DVD/CD-RW
Drive (Q:)

The letter of the drive is written under the icon. If it is a letter other than Q, then replace Q in the Run dialogue box, with the relevant letter (see Section 4, Action 2).

Action 3

If the disk still does not run, try phoning the helpline found inside the disk packaging in the front of the CD. (Check how much they charge per minute before you call.)

Section 5:
Loading and Running Computer Games on CD

Action 1

Load the CD. Most games will Autorun. Once the game is loaded just follow the instructions on the screen and you can start.

For more on Games see *Chapter Four: How to play Computer Games.*

Playing Music and Videos

A music CD or video DVD will Autorun on Windows Media Player. For more details on Windows Media Player see Chapter Twelve.

Section 6:
Copying Files or Folders onto CD-R or CD-RW

Action 1

Insert a blank CD into the disk drive. The **CD Drive** dialogue box opens (Fig. 2) Select **Open** and then click **OK.**

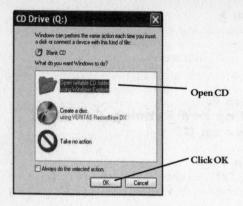

Fig. 2

Action 2

The **CD Drive** window opens.

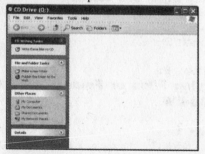

Fig. 3

Action 3

Click on **My Computer** and the My Computer window opens window opens (Fig. 4)

You need to find the file or folder that you wish to copy. Double–click on the drive where you have previously saved your work, i.e. HDD (C:) or floppy.

Fig. 4

Action 4

Locate and highlight your file or folder.

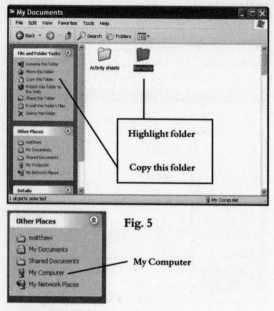

Fig. 5

Fig.6

Action 5

Click on **Copy this folder** or **Copy this file** (if you are copying a picture a pane will appear on the left of the window, entitled **Picture Tasks)**. Click on **Copy to CD** and the **Copy Items** dialogue box opens (Fig. 7). Select **CD Drive** and click on the **Copy** button.

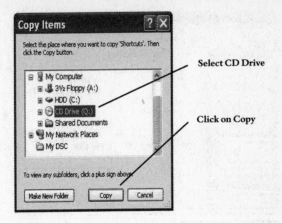

Fig. 7

Action 6

In the **Other Places** pane click on **My Computer** (Fig. 5 and Fig. 6).

Double click on the CD drive and the CD Drive window opens (Fig. 8) showing a temporary area where the files ready to be written to the CD are held.

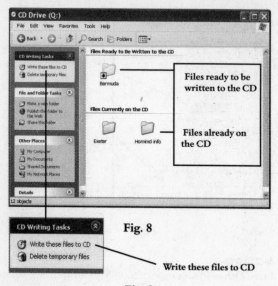

Fig. 8

Fig. 9

Action 4

Under the pane called **CD Writing Tasks**, click on **Write these files to CD**. The Writing Wizard will then be displayed.

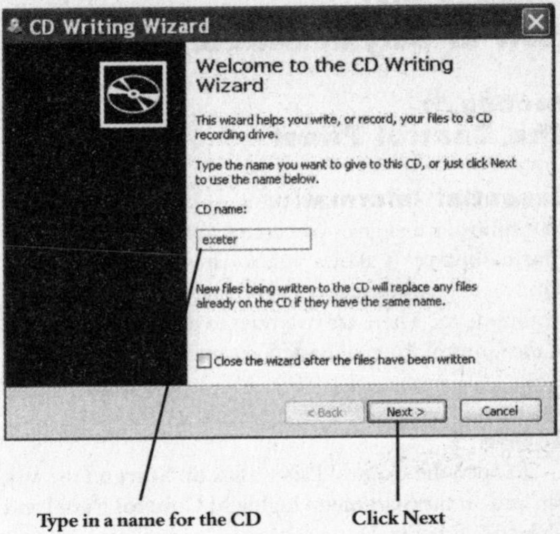

Type in a name for the CD   Click Next

Fig. 10

Action 6

Type in a name for your CD and then click on **Next>** and
follow the instructions as they appear.

Chapter Six:
How to Stay in Control of Your PC

Section 1:
The Control Panel

Essential Information

The control panel gives you access to many functions on your computer. It allows you to alter settings, add and remove programs, and generally change things to suit your requirements. There are two ways to display the contents of the Control Panel, Classic View and Category View.

Action 1

To open the Control Panel, click on **Start** on the task bar, and on the Start menu highlight **Control Panel** and click once (see Fig. 1).

Fig. 1

This will open the Control Panel window as shown in Figure 2. It will probably open in Category View.

Back button

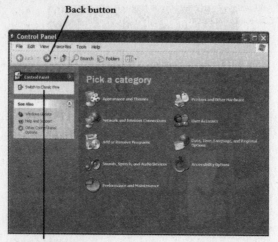

Switch to Classic View

Fig. 2

Action 2
Category View

The different functions of the computer have been grouped together into various categories to allow you ease of access. Pick any category and double-click to open. Discover and view the contents and then return to the main Control Panel window by clicking on the **Back** button.

Action 3
Classic View

Click on the **Switch to Classic View** link.

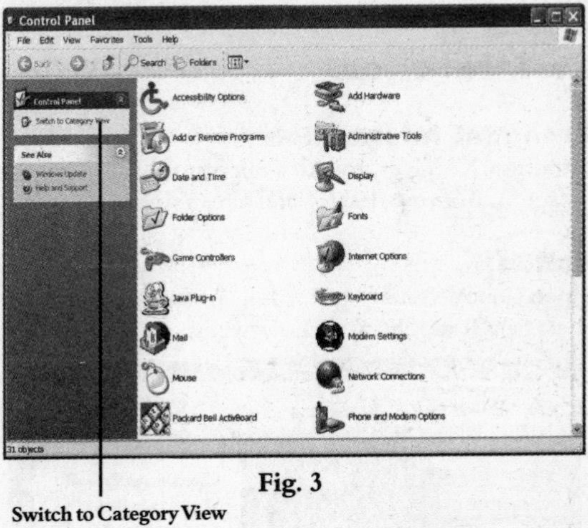

Fig. 3

Switch to Category View

The various functions of the Control Panel are listed separately, with their individual icons. Sometimes it is quicker to find an item in Classic View rather than go through the subdivisions of Category View. To open a program, simply click on the relevant icon. If you wish to return to Category View, click on the **Switch to Category View** link.

Action 4

To close the Control Panel window, click on the **Close** box.

Section 2:
Desktop Styles

Essential Information

Windows XP gives you the opportunity to alter the background of your desktop and screen saver.

Action 1

Open Control Panel (as in Section 1). Click on Appearance and Themes and a new window opens.

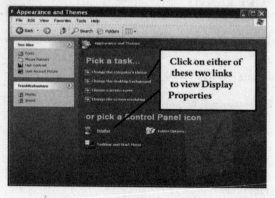

Fig. 4

Action 2

There are two ways of opening up Display Properties.

1. Either **Pick a task** and click on Change the desktop background.
2. Or **pick a Control Panel icon** and click on the Display icon.

Whichever you choose, the **Display Properties** dialogue box will open (Fig. 4). (You can also open this box by choosing to view Control Panel in Classic View and clicking on the Display icon.)

Action 3

Click on the tab called **Desktop.** Look at Figure 5. Notice the small monitor where you can see a preview of the desktop background selection.

Background gives you a variety of desktop options. Use the scroll bar to find a background that appeals to you, click on the name and a preview will show on the small monitor. Once you have found a background that you wish to keep, click on the downward pointing arrow by **Position,** and from the drop-down list, select either tile, center or stretch. **Tile** will repeat the image across the whole desktop as a series of tiles. **Center** will set a part of the style in the centre of the screen only. **Stretch** can be used to make a picture fit the screen. Once you have made your selection, click on **Apply** and then **OK.** Close all the open windows to return to the desktop and view your choice.

Desktop tab ——

Position drop-down list
Stretch, Tile or Center

Preview Monitor ——

Background ——

Customize Desktop ——

Click on arrow for
colour options ——

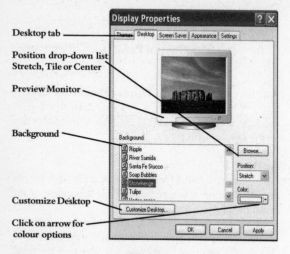

Fig. 5

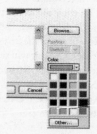

Fig. 6

Action 4

As an alternative to the set backgrounds you could choose a plain colour background or a picture from your own collection. On backgrounds, highlight **[None]** and then click on the arrow by **Color** and a drop-down palette gives you a choice of plain backgrounds (Fig. 6).

Select one and preview it on the small monitor, then click on **Apply** and **OK**. To choose a picture from your own files, click on the **Browse** button, once you have made a selection choose from **Position** as in Action 3, click on **Apply** and **OK**. Close all the open windows to return to your desktop and view your choice.

Section 3:
Customising the Desktop

Essential Information

It is possible to change the icons on you desktop and also the Desktop cleanup facility allows you to remove any icons which you haven't used for 60 days. You are given the option of whether to retain or remove them and the date that they were last used, if ever. If removed, the icons are placed in a folder and can be returned to the desktop, should they be required at a later date.

Action 1

Click on **Customize Desktop** (Fig. 5) and the **General** tab will be displayed (Fig. 7). If you wish to clean up your desktop, click on **Clean Desktop Now.**

Click on the icon
you wish to change

Click on Change
Icon

Click on Clean
Desktop Now

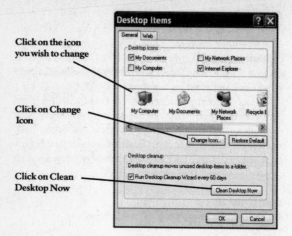

Fig. 7

Action 2

Follow the instructions of the cleanup wizard as they appear
on the screen.

Action 3

To change an icon, selecting from those in the middle of
the general tab, click on the one you wish to change and
then click on **Change Icon.**

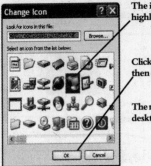

The icon in current use will be highlighted

Click on your new choice of icon and then click OK

The new icon will be placed on your desktop, replacing the previous one

Fig. 8

Section 4:
Customising the Screen Saver

Action 1

Open up Display Properties . Click on the Screen Saver tab (Fig. 9) or under **Pick a task**, (on the Control Panel) click on **Choose a screen saver**.

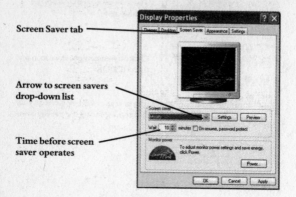

Fig. 9

Action 2

The monitor at the top of this window gives you a preview of the selection. To change the screen saver, click once on the downward pointing arrow in the section called **Screen Saver** and a list of other screen savers titles will be displayed (Fig. 10).

Drop-down list of
screen saver styles

Settings button

Preview button

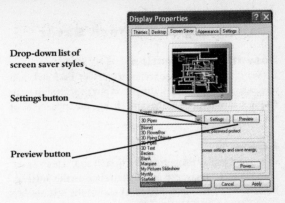

Fig. 10

Click on one that appeals and it will be previewed on the small monitor. The wait time before the screen saver actually operates can also be changed.

In the box entitled **Wait** there are two arrows pointing up and down. Use these to increase or decrease the time before the screen saver operates. When you have completed your selections click on **Apply** and then **OK.**

Top Tip

It is probably a good idea to have the screen saver 'wait time' set for at least 5 minutes. It can become very irritating if the screen disappears every time you pause for thought!

Section 5:
Customising the Screen Saver

Essential Information
It's very easy to customise your screen saver. Each style will have a slightly different settings box but they all allow you to select various options that will change the appearance of the basic format.

Action 1
Open up Display Properties (Section 2) and Screen Saver. Choose a screen saver style and then click on the **Settings** button. As an example, Figure 11 shows the settings box for the style called 3D Pipes. There are options for changing the speed, the pipe and surface styles and the number of pipes!

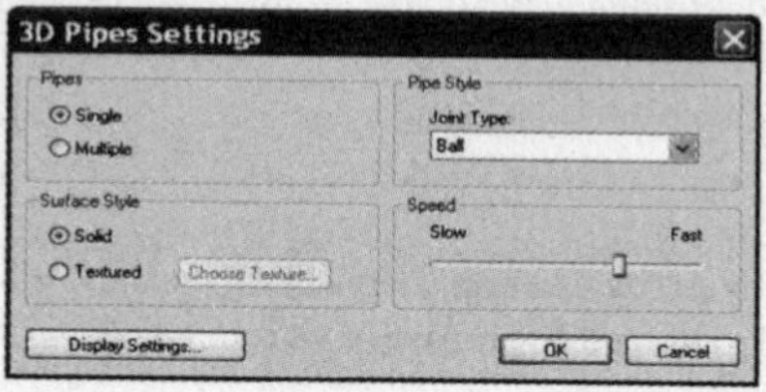

Fig. 11

Figure 12 shows another example which is slightly different. Here, the settings box for the **Marquee Setup** allows you to type in text, choose a background colour and speed. You can also format the text by clicking on the **Format Text** box.

Fig. 12

Action 2

Once you have made your settings selections for a screen
saver style, click on the **OK** button and you are returned to
Display Properties.

Action 3

Click on the **Preview** button and the screen saver will be
displayed across the full screen for a few seconds. If you
decide to keep your selection then click on **Apply** and then
OK.

Section 6:
Appearance and Themes: Style, Fonts and Colour

Essential Information

There are two further tabs on the Display Properties box
which will enable you to personalize the appearance of

your computer. These tabs allow you to choose such things as colour, style and the size of fonts. If you have been used to working on previous editions of Windows, and wish to continue using the earlier style, you can select Windows Classic as the theme.

Action 1

Open up Display Properties and select the **Themes** tab. Click on the arrow by **Theme** and a drop down list displays all the theme options (Fig. 13).

If you wish to remain with the Windows XP style make sure that you select that option. If you wish to use the earlier style of previous editions, click on Windows Classic.

Themes tab ———

Themes drop-down list ———

Preview screen ———

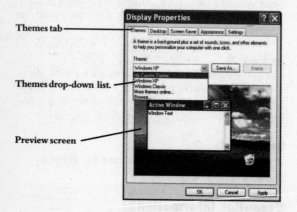

Fig. 13

A preview of the theme will be displayed in the small screen on the Display Properties box. Once you have decided upon your choice of theme, click on **Apply** and then **OK**.

Action 2

Select the **Appearance** tab (Fig. 14). This allows you to choose colour style and font size. To change the size of the fonts, click on the arrow by **Font size**, and a drop-down list will display the three options. In the same way you can change the colour scheme or the style of the windows and buttons. The preview screen will display the changes as you select them. When you have decided upon your selections, click on **Apply** and then **OK**.

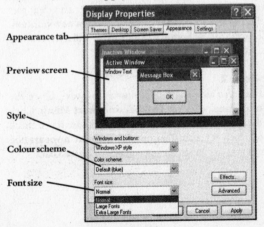

Fig. 14

Section 7:
Moving and Hiding the Taskbar

Essential Information
The taskbar is the strip that runs along the bottom of the screen and programs that are currently running, appear on it as buttons. This allows you to see at a glance which programs are open and to recall them to the screen by clicking on the relevant program button on the taskbar.

Action 1
Although the taskbar usually sits along the bottom of the screen it can be moved to any of the four sides of the screen. To do this, simply place the pointer on a clear part of the bar and then click and drag it to its new position. Release the mouse button and the taskbar will remain where you have placed it.

Action 2
You can also alter the taskbar in various ways. Open the Control Panel, click on **Taskbar and Start Menu.** Click on the tab called **Taskbar** (Fig. 15). There are seven check boxes, each set against an option. **Taskbar appearance** allows you to change the appearance of the taskbar.

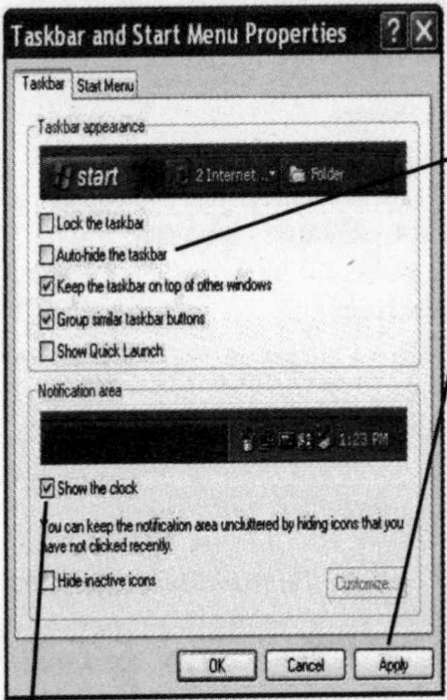

Click on the check box
by Auto-hide the
taskbar, and ensure a
tick is present.

Click on Apply and then
OK. The taskbar will
now be hidden from
view except when you
move the mouse over
the area of the screen
where it is normally
placed

To reverse Auto-hide,
simply remove the tick
from the check box.
Click on Apply and then
OK.

Show the clock

Fig. 15

Action 3
The **Notification area** allows you to choose whether or
not to have the computer clock visible. To show the clock,
make sure there is a tick in the check box.

Action 4
To read more about possible changes to the taskbar use the
What's This? (see *Chapter Three: How to use Microsoft Help*).

Action 5

If you decide to change any options, remember, make sure a tick is present or removed from the relevant check box. Then click **Apply** and **OK**.

Section 8:
Customising the Start Menu

Essential Information

The Start button, which sits on the taskbar, provides you with the pathway into your PC and its programs. It is possible to customise the Start menu to suit your own requirements. To do this you need to open **Taskbar and Start Menu Properties**.

Action 1

Open the Control Panel, click on **Appearance and themes** and then, click on **Taskbar and Start Menu**. Click on the tab called **Start Menu**. The two radio buttons allow you to select from the Windows XP Start menu or the Classic Start menu which was used in previous Windows editions. As you select a different radio button, the style will appear in the preview box (Fig. 16).

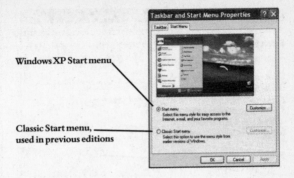

Fig. 16

Action 2

To further customise your Start menu, click on the **Customize** button. The **General** tab allows you to select large or small icons or to decide on how many program shortcuts you wish to be visible on the Start menu.

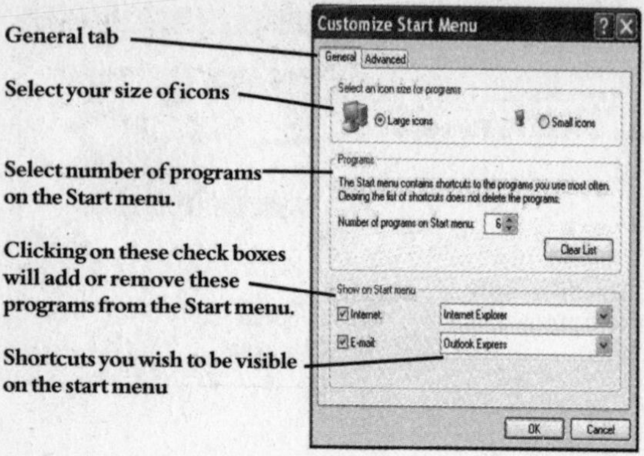
General tab
Select your size of icons
Select number of programs on the Start menu.
Clicking on these check boxes will add or remove these programs from the Start menu.
Shortcuts you wish to be visible on the start menu
Customize Start Menu
General
Advanced
Select an icon size for programs
Large icons
Small icons
Programs
The Start menu contains shortcuts to the programs you use most often. Clearing the list of shortcuts does not delete the programs.
Number of programs on Start menu:
6
Clear List
Show on Start menu
Internet:
Internet Explorer
E-mail:
Outlook Express
OK
Cancel

Fig. 17

Action 3

Click on the **Advanced** tab. This lists a number of useful functions which you can activate by clicking on the check box or radio button. You may find **Recent Documents** especially useful.

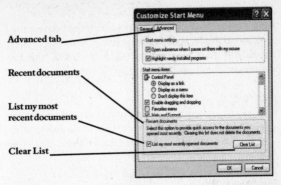

Advanced tab

Recent documents

List my most recent documents

Clear List

Fig. 18

Click on the check box and tick **List my most recent documents**. Now, as you create documents, they will be listed for your convenience on the Documents menu, which can be accessed from the Start menu.

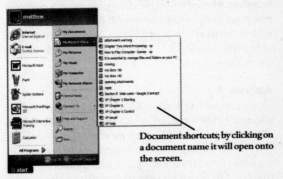

Document shortcuts; by clicking on a document name it will open onto the screen.

Fig. 19

Action 4

After a while the list of recent documents can become very long and it may be a good idea to clear it. To do this click on the **Clear List** button, and then click OK and the documents menu will be cleared (Fig. 18).

Action 5

When you have finished making your Start menu selections, click **OK**. To read more about changes to the Start menu, use the **What's This?** help (see *Chapter Three: How to use Microsoft Help*).

Section 9:
Sounds and Audio Devices:
Changing Sounds

Essential Information

Windows XP enables you to change the sounds that your computer makes while performing its various operations, such as closing or opening a program. You will need speakers or headphones attached to your computer in order to hear any of these sounds.

Action 1

Open Control Panel, select **Sounds and Audio Devices** and under **Pick a task** select **change the sound scheme**. The **Sounds and Audio Devices Properties** dialogue box will be displayed. Under **Program Events** you will see a list of events with tiny pictures of loudspeakers next to them. The ones with loudspeakers already have sounds

attached to them. The name of the sound is shown in the
Sounds box .

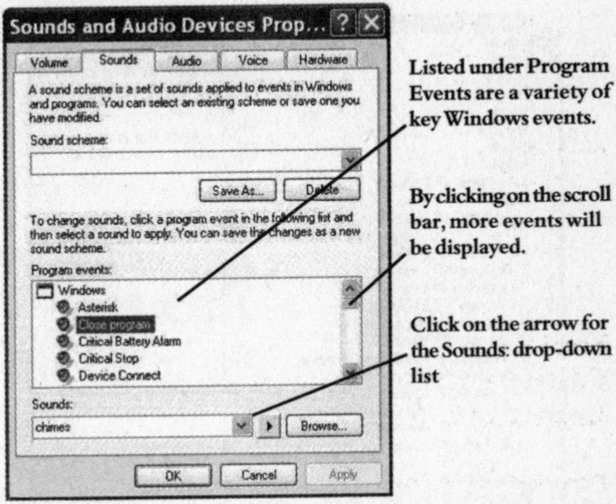

Listed under Program Events are a variety of key Windows events.

By clicking on the scroll bar, more events will be displayed.

Click on the arrow for the Sounds: drop-down list

Fig. 20

Action 2

Highlight an event. If it has a loudspeaker next to it, the
name of the sound will be in the **Sounds** box. If it does not
have a loud speaker alongside it, then **[None]** will be in
the Sounds box.

Action 3

Click once on the **Sounds** downward pointing arrow and
a drop-down list of sounds is displayed. Select the sound
that you wish to accompany the selected Windows

operation. Figure 21 shows that we have chosen **chimes** from the list.

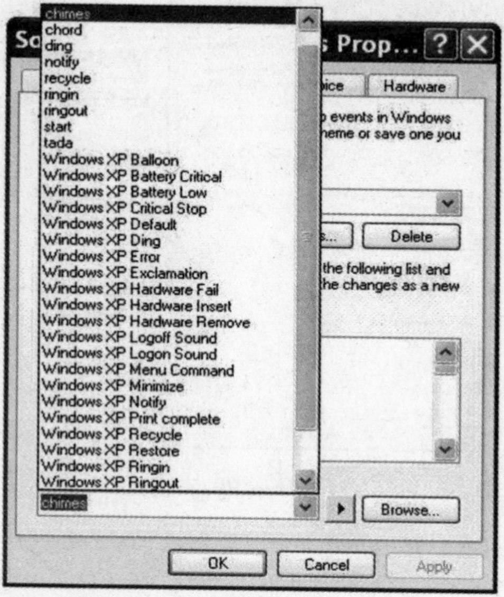

Fig. 21

Action 4

Click on **Apply** at the bottom of the box, then **OK**, and the sound will play whenever that particular action is performed.

Top Tip
Sounds are great fun and can act as useful reminders. Resist the temptation however to allocate a sound to as many things as you can - they will cease to be effective as an alert.

Action 5
To Remove Sounds

Open up Sound and Audio Devices Properties as you did in Action 1. Highlight the relevant event. In the Sounds box, click on the downward pointing arrow to get the drop-down list of sounds. Highlight **[None]**, then click on **Apply** and **OK.** The sound has now been removed.

Section 10:
Sounds and Audio Devices: Volume Control

Action 1

Click on the **Volume** tab of the Sounds and Audio Devices Properties dialogue box.

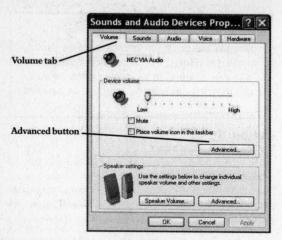

Fig. 22

Action 2

Click on the **Advanced** button and the **Volume Control**
window opens (Fig. 23). Drag the slider to increase or
decrease volume. It's probably a good idea to leave the other
options for the device to sort out.

Volume Control —
Slider —

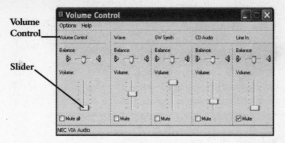

Fig. 23

Action 3

You can also open Volume Control by clicking on the Start menu, All Programs, Accessories, Entertainment and then Volume Control.

Top Tip
Don't forget that you also have volume controls on your speakers. These are usually buttons which you can turn manually to increase or decrease sound. If using the volume control above does not improve the sound, try the speaker controls.

Section 11:
The Mouse

Essential Information
The Mouse Properties dialogue box allows you to alter the mouse buttons (useful if you are left-handed), the scroll wheel (if your mouse has one) and to change the style of the pointers.

Action 1
Open the Control Panel. Click on **Printers and Other Hardware**. Under Pick a Control Panel, click on **Mouse** icon and the **Mouse Properties** dialogue box opens.

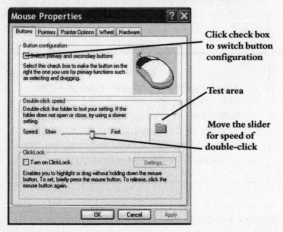

Click check box to switch button configuration

Test area

Move the slider for speed of double-click

Fig. 24

Action 2

Notice that there are **five tabs.** Click on the tab for **Buttons.**
The **Button configuration** allows you to switch the
functions of the mouse buttons. Click on the check box
with the **left-hand** mouse button. The functions of the
buttons are switched as indicated by the button colour
change. This is useful if you are left-handed.

Action 3

To switch the button back, click on the check box using
the **right-hand** button, and the colour of the mouse
button reverts to original.

If you are right-handed, make sure that you leave the
check box unactivated. Click on **Apply**, then **OK.**

Top Tip

If you are left-handed and you alter the mouse
buttons, you must remember to reverse any
further instructions regarding left or right
mouse buttons.

Action 3

The **double-click speed** and test area are covered in
Chapter One: How to Get Started.

Section 12:
Mouse Wheels

Your mouse may have a central wheel between the two

buttons. This wheel allows you to scroll through a page
without having to click onto the scrolling bar. The **Wheel**
tab on Mouse Properties enables you to alter the amount
that the wheel scrolls at any one time.

Action 1

Click on the **Wheel** tab. If you are happy with the current
rate of scroll, leave the number unchanged. If not, then
the upward and downward pointing arrows allow you to
increase or decrease the number of lines scrolled for every
notch of the mouse wheel. Click on **Apply** and then **OK**.

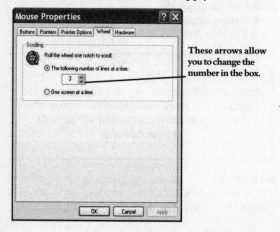

These arrows allow
you to change the
number in the box.

Fig. 25

Section 13:
Customising the Pointer

Action 1
Click on the tab marked **Pointers**.

Scheme ————

Preview window
of scheme chosen ————

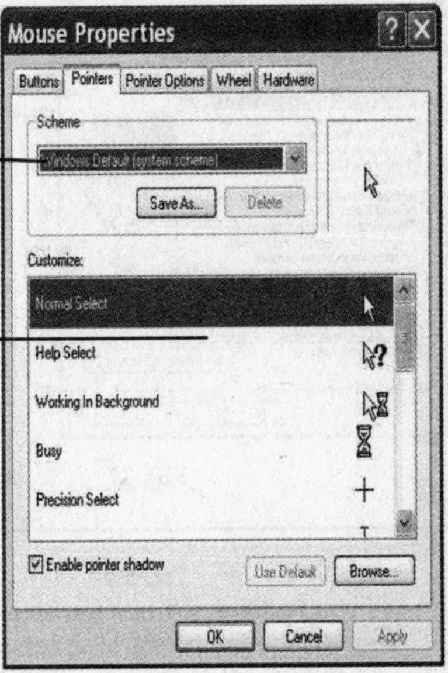

Fig. 26

Click on the arrow by **Scheme** and a drop-down list will

allow you to select different styles of pointers. When you
have chosen a style, click on **Apply** and then **OK**.

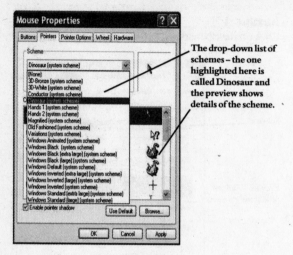

The drop-down list of
schemes – the one
highlighted here is
called Dinosaur and
the preview shows
details of the scheme.

Fig. 27

Top Tip
If you find the pointers too small, select
Magnified from the list of schemes and the
pointers will change to a larger size.

Action 2

Click on the tab called **Pointer Options**. By adjusting the sliders (using click and drag), it is possible to vary the pointer speed and trail. If you wish to experiment with the pointer trail, click the check box next to **Display pointer trails** so that it shows a tick.

Action 3

Move the slider between short and long (Fig. 28). As you do so, the pointer will leave a trail. Decide whether you want to see a long trail or a short one and when you are happy with your choice, click on **Apply** and then **OK**.

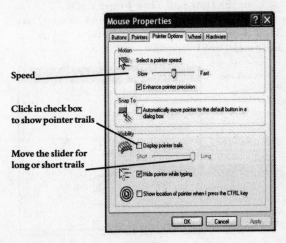

Fig. 28

Section 14:
Altering the Date and Time

Essential Information

It's very easy to adjust the date and time on your computer. This function is particularly useful when you are travelling and need to alter your laptop computer. The **Date and Time Properties** dialogue box enables you to make any necessary adjustments.

Action 1

If the clock is visible on your taskbar, simply double-click on it and the **Date and Time Properties** dialogue box will open. If not, click on **Control Panel**, then on **Date, Time, Language and Regional Options**, and then on **Date and Time Properties**.

Month and year boxes

Digital time box

Current time zone status

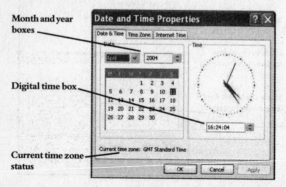

Fig. 29

Action 2

To change the time, alter the digital time in the box directly beneath the clock. To do this click in the box and highlight a pair of numbers, i.e. hours, minutes or seconds, and using the upward and downward pointing arrows change the numbers as required. The clock face will follow. Click **Apply** then **OK**.

Action 3

To the left of the clock is a calendar and above it are two boxes. One shows the month and the other the year. By clicking on the arrows to the right of the boxes you can change the month and year. Click **Apply** then **OK**.

Section 15:
Altering the Time Zone

Action 1

Click on the tab **Time Zone**.

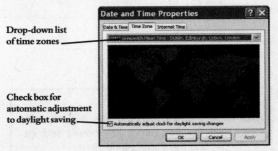

Drop-down list of time zones

Check box for automatic adjustment to daylight saving

Fig. 30

Action 2

Click on the **Time Zone** drop-down list and all the world's time zones are displayed. Click on the time zone that is applicable to you and then click on **Apply** and **OK**. The computer clock will change automatically to its new setting.

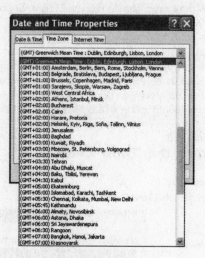

Fig. 31

Top Tip
After experimenting with the time and calendar make sure that you return it to today's settings and the correct time zone.

Section 16:
Keyboard Properties

Essential Information
This function allows you to dictate the pace at which letters appear on the screen and the rate at which the cursor blinks.

Action 1
Open Control Panel, click on **Printers and Other Hardware**, and then on **Keyboard.** The **Keyboard Properties** dialogue box has three tabs (Fig. 32). Choose the tab that says **Speed**.

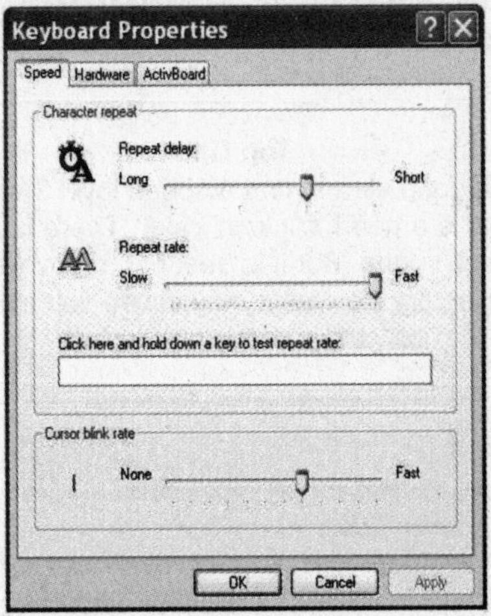

Fig. 32

Action 2

Look at the first section called **Character repeat** and within
that section, **Repeat rate.** This speedometer dictates how
fast the letters come up on the screen. Move the indicator
right down to slow. Now click in the white text box and
hold down a key and notice the speed at which it is repeated.
Very slow! Return the indicator to a sensible repeat level or
to one that you find comfortable.

Action 3

Look at the **Cursor blink rate.** Change the speed from
where it is at the moment right up to fast. Notice how the
speed of the cursor has increased. Move the slider until you
find a satisfactory cursor blink rate.

Top Tip

It is a good idea to find a speed level that **you**
feel is a good 'blinking' rate. There is no
'correct' speed. But it is best not to have a rate
that is very slow as it may cause you to lose
the cursor amongst the text.

Action 4

When you are happy with your choice of speed click on
Apply and then **OK.**

Section 17:
Adding a Program

Action 1

Place the disk into the correct slot and gently push it into the machine. If it does not start straight away try opening the **Control Panel** and click on **Add or Remove Programs**.

Action 2

A new window opens called Add or Remove Programs. Click on the **Add New Progams** button.

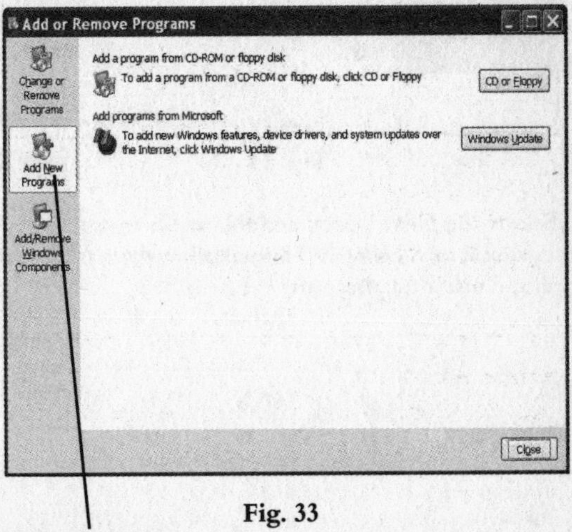

Fig. 33

Add New Programs

Action 3

Click on the **CD or Floppy** button. The **Install Program from Floppy Disk or CD-ROM** window is displayed.

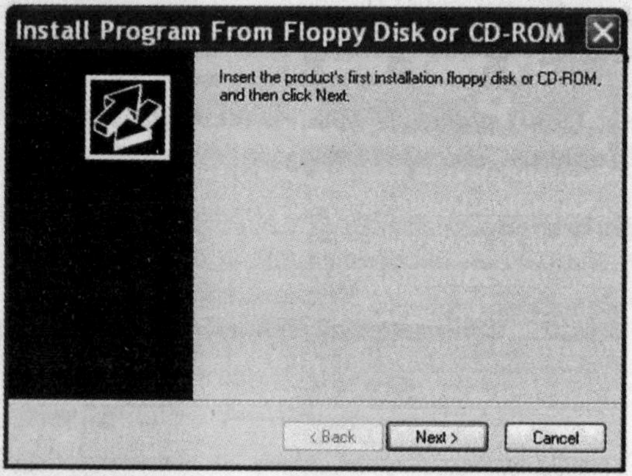

Fig. 34

Click on the **Next** button and follow the instructions as they appear on the screen. This will allow the computer to find and install the program.

Section 18:
Removing a Program

Essential Information

When you install a program onto your hard drive it will sit there taking up space until you decide to use it. If this program is a game, it can use up a large amount of memory. If you keep adding programs, eventually the hard disk will become full.

Top Tip
It's a good idea to remove programs as soon as they become unwanted or before installing a new program.

Action 1

To remove a program open **Add or Remove Programs**. Click on the **Change or Remove Programs** button.

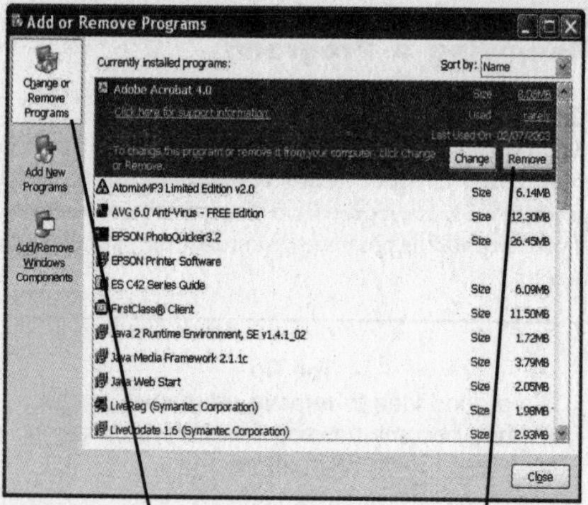

Fig. 35

Change or Remove Programs   Remove button

Highlight the program that you want to delete and click once on the **Remove** button.

Action 2

One of two things will now happen.

1. A box will open called **Confirm File Deletion**. It will ask if you are sure that you wish to delete this program. If you are, then click on **Yes** and the computer will remove the program. If you are unsure, click **No**.

2. Alternatively, an **Uninstall Wizard** may open. Simply follow the instructions as they appear on the screen to remove the program.

Top Tip
Beware! Once the computer has deleted a program there is no way of getting it back except by reinstalling the program from floppy disk or CD.

Section 19
Viewing Fonts

Action 1
It is possible to view fonts by going opening up **Control Panel** and clicking on **Appearance and Themes**. Locate **See Also** and click on **Fonts**.

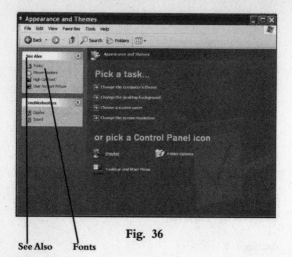

Fig. 36

See Also   Fonts

Action 2

The **Fonts** window opens. Each icon represents a different font. Double-click on one and an example of the font will be displayed. Close the Font window by clicking on the Close box.

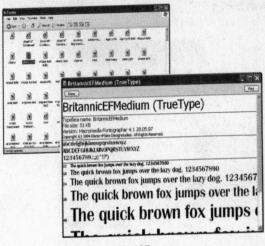

Fig. 37

Section 20:
Using Search

Essential Information

Search is a very useful tool in helping you to trawl through the computer memory to find lost files. Because we are human and not pieces of high tech electronic equipment we all make mistakes. For example it is very easy to save a file accidentally in the wrong place. The problem is, where? Another common problem is forgetting the exact name of the file as well as its location.

Action 1

Click on the **Start** button and click on **Search**.

Fig. 38

The **Search Results** window is displayed.

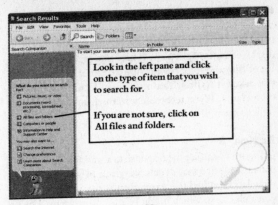

Look in the left pane and click on the type of item that you wish to search for.

If you are not sure, click on All files and folders.

Fig. 39

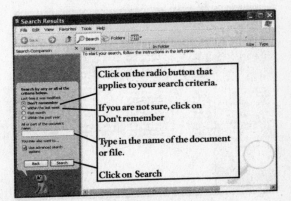

Click on the radio button that applies to your search criteria.

If you are not sure, click on Don't remember

Type in the name of the document or file.

Click on Search

Fig. 40

Action 2

The program will now search through the computer's memory. Once it has located the document or file it will be displayed in the right pane. It may also present you with a list of files and folders with similar names to the one that you asked it to find. You must then decide which is the correct one. If you recognise it immediately, double-click on it to open. If not, go onto Action 3.

Action 3

In Figure 41 can see the response to a search for a file called cookies. Notice that details are given of when the items were last modified (i.e. worked on) – this will help to give you a clue as to which might be the correct item. The list also tells you what type of files they are and where the files or folders have been saved.

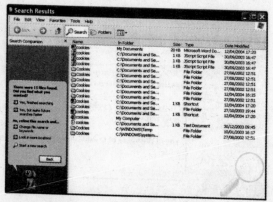

Fig. 41

Action 4

Sometimes you may need to expand the headings such as
In Folder or **Date Modified** in order to read all the words.
To do this, simply place the pointer onto the fine line
between the headings. The pointer changes to a black cross
with two arrowheads.

Fig. 42

This will allow you to resize the headings in the direction
of the arrows. Click and hold down the left mouse button
and drag the line to the right. All the headings can be
resized (made wider or narrower) in this way.

Decide upon which document you wish to open and
then double click on it.

Section 21:
Creating Shortcuts

It is very easy to create shortcuts to programs and files
which you frequently use. The shortcut will be in the
form of an icon, which will sit on your desktop. By moving
the pointer onto the icon and double clicking, you will be
taken straight into the program or file without having to
navigate the usual pathway.

You can create shortcuts from a number of the Microsoft
Windows and it is the same procedure for all of them. Here
are four examples.

Windows Explorer

Open **Windows Explorer (Start, All Programs)**. On the right pane of Windows Explorer, highlight the file or folder which requires a shortcut. In Figure 43, for example, a folder called 'watermarks' is shown as highlighted.

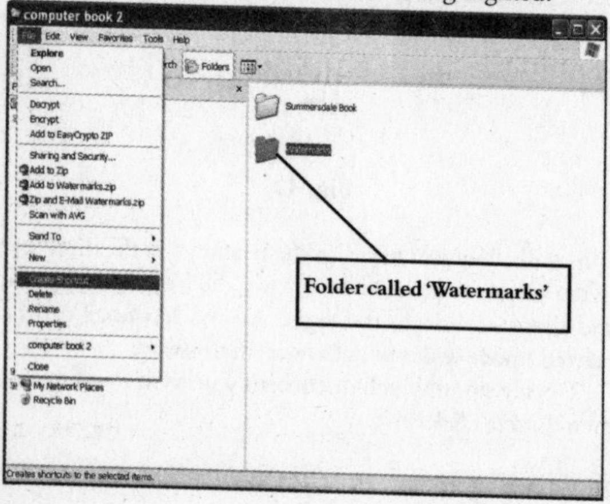

Fig. 43

Click on **File** and then click on **Create shortcut** on the drop-down menu. A new icon will appear on the right pane entitled **Shortcut to...** and then the name of the folder.

In Figure 44, for example, there is now a shortcut called **Shortcut to Watermarks**.

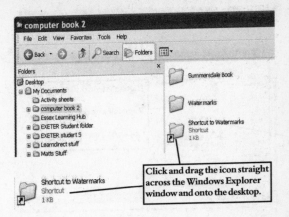

Click and drag the icon straight across the Windows Explorer window and onto the desktop.

Fig. 44

If not enough of the desktop is visible for you to do this then click on the title bar of the window and drag it to one side, thus revealing more desktop. For more on Windows Explorer see *Chapter Seven: How to Create and Manage Files*.

Close Windows Explorer.

Microsoft Word

Open **Word** and drag the page down the screen so that part of the Desktop is visible. Click on **Open** and locate the relevant file or folder which requires a shortcut. Left click on the file or folder, and then without moving the mouse, right click.

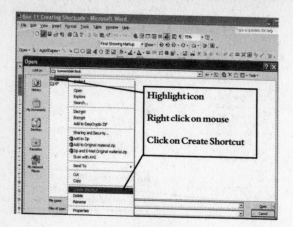

Fig. 45

A drop-down menu will be displayed. Move the pointer down the menu and click on **Create shortcut**. A new icon will appear in the Open box entitled **Shortcut to...** and then the name of the folder.

Highlight the shortcut you have just created and click and drag it onto the visible part of the desktop.

Control Panel
Control Panel is another window where shortcuts can be created.

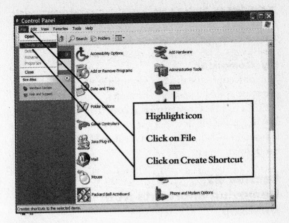

Fig. 46

Depending on the program that you have selected the following box may appear.

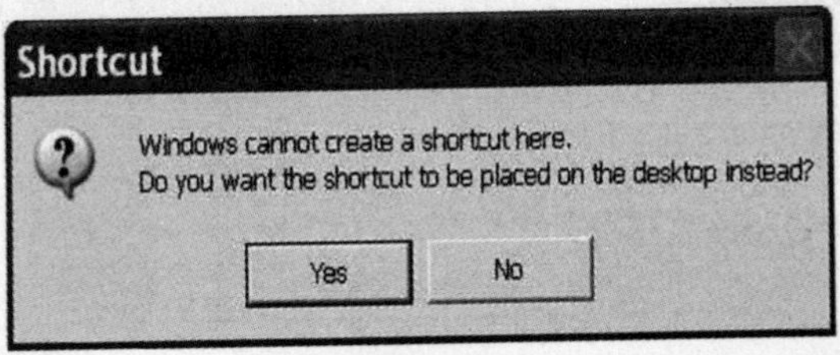

Fig. 47

If you click on **Yes** the shortcut will be placed directly onto the desktop and you will not need to click and drag it across.

My Computer

The procedure for the My Computer window is exactly the same as in the previous examples.

Open **My Computer** (from the Start menu). Highlight the file or folder for which you wish to create a shortcut. Click on **File**, select **Create Shortcut** from the drop-down menu.

Section 22:
Removing Shortcuts from your Desktop

Action 1

Make sure you are looking at the PC desktop.

Action 2

Click once on the shortcut to be deleted and it will change colour. Click on the *right button* of the mouse and a drop-down menu will appear as in Figure 48.

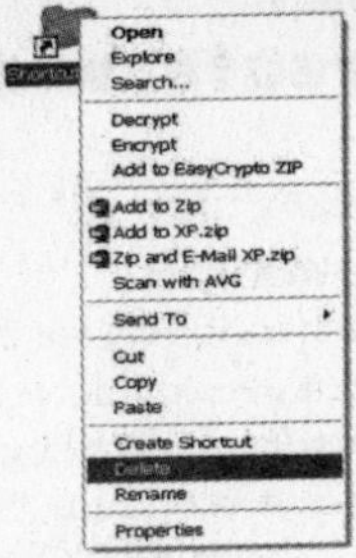

Fig. 48

Click on the word **Delete** and a **Confirm File Delete** message box will appear on the screen.

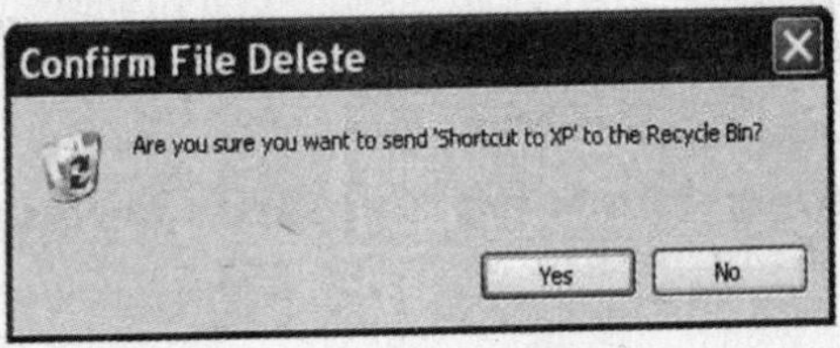

Fig. 49

Action 3

Click on **Yes** and the shortcut will be removed from the desktop. It's only the shortcut icon on the desktop that has been deleted; not the actual program or file, which can still be reached in the usual way.

Chapter Seven:
How to Create and Manage Files

Essential Information

As you accumulate more data on your PC, it is essential to begin to your manage files and folders in a deliberate and logical way. **Windows Explorer** allows you to view the contents of disks and folders on hard disk, floppy disk and CD, and to create your own folders. This facility will enable you to organise and manage information and work more effectively. Explorer can be opened by going to My Computer or My Documents on the Start menu or by clicking on All Programs and then Windows Explorer. The following section will use My Computer as an illustration, but try the other ways once you have mastered this one.

Section 1:
Finding Windows Explorer through My Computer

Action 1

Click on the **Start** button and open the Start menu.

How to Create and Manage Files

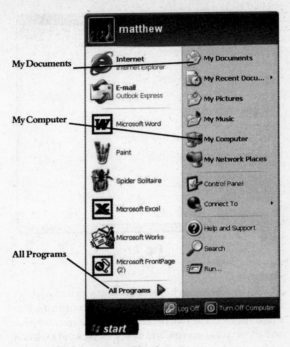

Fig. 1

Action 2

Highlight **My Computer** and click once. The **My Computer** window opens.

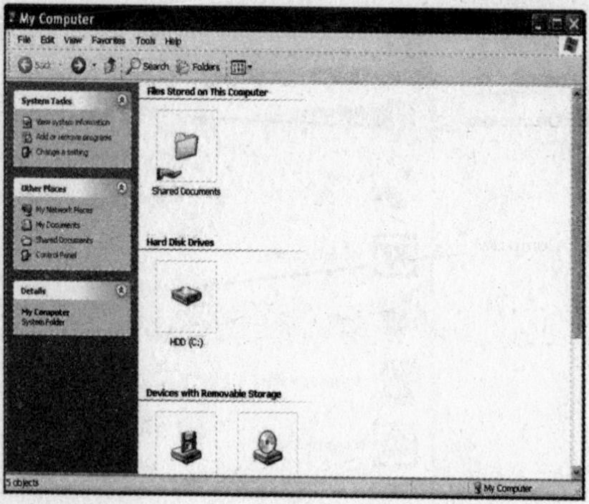

Fig. 2

Action 3

The folder structure is hierarchical, so one main folder can contain sub-folders which in turn may contain further folders or files. The functions on the toolbar and menu bar will allow you to navigate and view your files and folders at various levels. Identify these functions on My Computer (Fig. 3).

Back/Forward: These will allow you to move between the folders that you have previously opened.
Up one level: If you are viewing a sub-folder this function will take you up to the folder above.

Search: This button opens the facility on Explorer which enables you to search for files and folders.

Folders: This opens and closes Windows Explorer.

View: This opens a drop-down menu which gives you different option of viewing the folders.

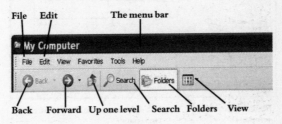

The Toolbar

Fig. 3

Action 4

Click on the **Folders** button.

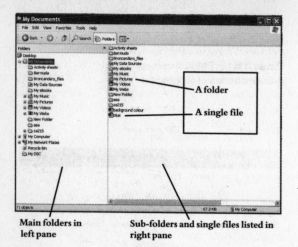

Main folders in left pane   Sub-folders and single files listed in right pane

Fig. 4

The Explorer bar has opened in the left pane and on the right pane are listed the sub-folders and files contained in the main folders (Fig. 4). Notice that files are not displayed on the left, only on the right of Explorer.

JArgon Buster
What's the difference between a file and a folder?
A file is a single document. A folder is larger than a file and is used to contain other folders and files.

Section 2:
Looking at Folders

Essential Information

Notice on the left of the window that there are folders or icons with a plus sign alongside them. This indicates that the folder or icon contains further objects. A folder with a minus sign means that it is already open and the contents will be listed below the folder in the left pane.

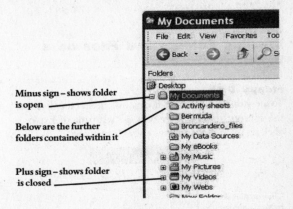

Minus sign – shows folder is open

Below are the further folders contained within it

Plus sign – shows folder is closed

Fig. 5

Action 1

Move the cursor to the plus sign next to My Documents and click once. The folder opens out and more folders are listed. By the side of My Documents is a minus sign showing that the folder is open (Fig. 5).

Action 2

Click on any folder and its contents will be displayed on the right pane.

Action 3

Click on the minus sign by My Documents and the folder will close.

Section 3:
Viewing Folders and Files on a Disk

Floppy Disk

To view the contents of a floppy disk, insert the disk into the appropriate disk drive. On the left pane of Explorer click on the plus sign next to **My Computer.**

Click on plus sign
by My Computer

Fig. 6

Click on **3½ Floppy (A:)** (Fig. 7) and the contents of the disk are displayed on the right side of Explorer.

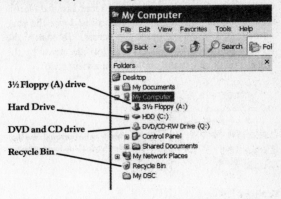

3½ Floppy (A) drive

Hard Drive

DVD and CD drive

Recycle Bin

Fig. 7

CD/DVD

To view the contents of a CD, insert the CD into the correct drive. On the left pane of Explorer click on the plus sign by **My Computer**. Click on **DVD/CD-RW Drive (Q:)**, (Fig. 7) and the contents of the disk are displayed on the right pane of Explorer.

Section 4:
Viewing Options for Files and Folders

Essential Information

There are various ways of viewing files and folders. It may, for example, be useful to view a picture file as a Thumbnail or Filmstrip, as the image can then be easily identified. If a large icon is needed, then opt for Tile view. List and Details display the file information as lists going down the page while icons, which are bigger, go across. To change the view of your files and folders click on the arrow by the **View** icon on the menu and click on a view style.

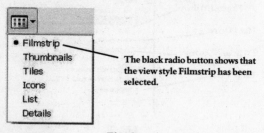

The black radio button shows that the view style Filmstrip has been selected.

Fig. 8

Section 5:
Creating and Naming Folders

Essential Information

As you create more files it is useful to organise those with a similar theme or topic into individual folders. Also if more than one person is using the same computer it is handy to create folders for each person's documents. Explorer can be used to create, delete and move folders.

Action 1

Open My Computer, click on **Folders** on the toolbar. In

the left pane of Explorer, click on **My Documents.** (Notice that the window has now changed name and become My Documents rather than My Computer.) Click on **File** on the menu bar and a drop-down menu appears (Fig. 9).

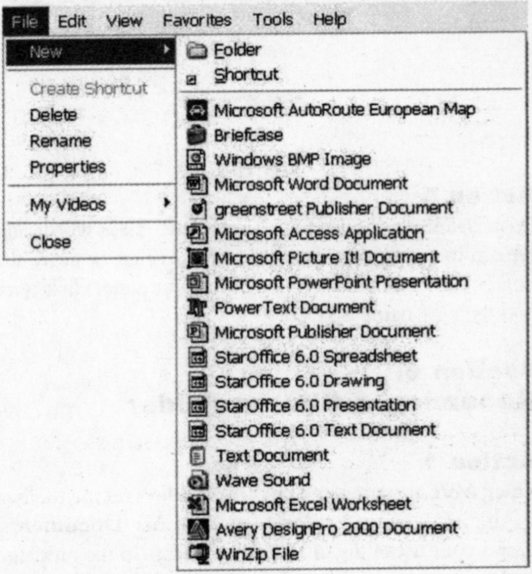

Fig. 9

Action 2

On the drop-down menu, move the cursor onto the word
New and another menu will appear. Move the cursor onto
the word **Folder**. A yellow folder will appear on the right
pane and labelled **New Folder**.

Fig. 10

Action 3

Press delete on the keyboard to remove these words and
type in the name of your choice. Press Enter or move the
cursor onto a blank section of the right pane, click once
and the new name is saved.

Section 6:
Renaming a File or Folder

Action 1

Open My Computer and click on **Folders** on the toolbar.
In the left pane of Explorer, click on **My Documents**.
Open your list of documents by clicking on the plus sign
by My Documents. Place the cursor onto the folder or file
to be renamed. Click on **File** on the menu bar and a drop-
down menu appears.

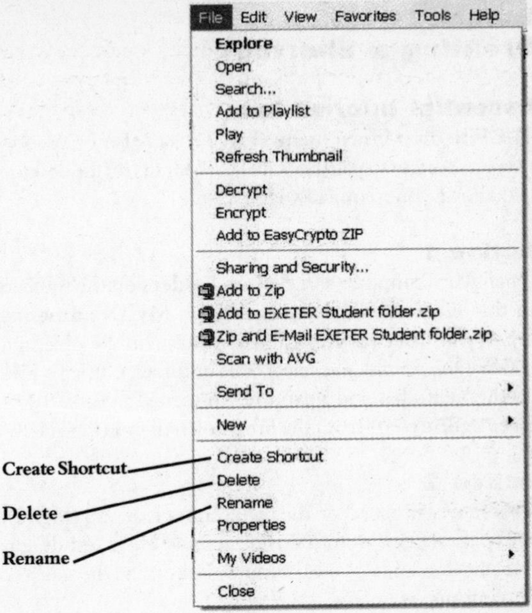

| File | Edit | View | Favorites | Tools | Help |

Explore
Open
Search...
Add to Playlist
Play
Refresh Thumbnail

Decrypt
Encrypt
Add to EasyCrypto ZIP

Sharing and Security...
Add to Zip
Add to EXETER Student folder.zip
Zip and E-Mail EXETER Student folder.zip
Scan with AVG

Send To ▸

New ▸

Create Shortcut
Delete
Rename
Properties

My Videos ▸

Close

Create Shortcut ——— Create Shortcut
Delete ——— Delete
Rename ——— Rename

Fig. 11

Click on the word **Rename**. The menu will then disappear and the text cursor will appear in the text box of the folder or file to be renamed. Delete the old name and then type in the new one. Press Enter and the new name is saved.

Section 7:
Creating a Shortcut

Essential Information
The **File** drop-down menu (Fig. 11) can also be used to create a shortcut to your document which sits on the desktop and allows you to quickly open it.

Action 1
Open My Computer and click on **Folders** on the toolbar. In the left pane of Explorer, click on **My Documents**. Open your list of documents by clicking on the plus sign by My Documents and select a file or folder. Click on **File** on the menu bar and a drop-down menu appears. Select **Create Shortcut** from the drop down menu (Fig. 11).

Action 2
A shortcut will appear on the right pane of Explorer (Fig.12). Move the cursor onto the shortcut and click and drag it onto the desktop. Release the mouse button and the shortcut remains in position on the desktop.

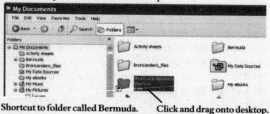

Shortcut to folder called Bermuda.   Click and drag onto desktop.

Fig. 12

Section 8:
Copying a File or Folder

Action 1
Open **My Computer**, click on **Folders** on the toolbar. In the left pane of Explorer, click on **My Documents**. Open your list of documents by clicking on the plus sign by My Documents and select a file or folder.

Action 2
Click on **Edit** on the menu bar and click on **Copy** on the drop-down menu.

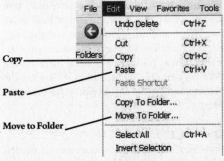

Fig. 13

Action 3
Click on the folder you wish to copy the item into. Click on **Edit** and on the drop-down menu click on **Paste** (Fig. 13).

Section 9:
Moving files into a Folder

Essential Information
You can use the Edit drop-down menu to move files and folders (Fig. 13) but a quicker way is to use 'drag and drop'.

Action 1
On the left side of Explorer locate the *folder* that you are going to use for housing your file.

Action 2
Locate the *file* on the right pane that you wish to place into the folder. Place the cursor on the file, click and hold down the left mouse button and you will be able to move the file. Drag the file onto the left pane. Carefully place it over the folder. When you have positioned the file correctly the selected folder becomes highlighted in blue. Release the left mouse button and the file will be placed (or dropped) into the folder.

Action 3
To check that the move has been successful, on the left pane of Explorer, click on the folder that has just received the file. The folder will open and the file should now be listed on the right pane.

Section 10:
Lost Files

Action 1
Don't panic if you think you have lost your file while trying to move it. Click on the Hard Drive – HDD (C:) – or Floppy (A:) on the left pane of Explorer and check to see whether the document is still listed on the right pane as a single document (still outside the folder). If it is, try moving it into the folder again.

Action 2
If you still cannot see the file then you may have place it accidentally into another folder. Don't worry – this will not harm any of the other programs or folders. Try opening up any of the folders which were in the immediate vicinity of the correct folder.

Action 3
If you still cannot find the file, ask the computer to find it for you. Read *Chapter Six: How to Stay in Control of Your PC*, Section 20, on searching for files.

Section 11:
Using the Right Mouse Button

Essential Information
You can also perform the procedures above by using the **right** mouse button. If you wish to create a new folder, rename a folder, delete, copy or move a folder or create a

shortcut, follow the same method above except instead of clicking on File or Edit on the menu bar click on the **right** mouse button. A drop-down menu will allow you to select the task you wish to perform. You can also use the right mouse button to do the above tasks on the **Open** or **Save As** windows. This is sometimes quicker than opening up My Documents or going into Explorer. When you are in an **Open** or **Save As** window, simply right click and a drop-down menu will allow you to select whichever task you wish to do.

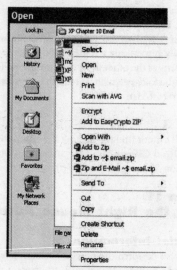

Fig. 14

Section 12:
Deleting Files

Essential Information

Using Explorer it is possible to delete files and folders from the Hard Disk (C:) and floppy disks.

Action 1

Open My Computer and click on **Folders** on the toolbar. In the left pane of Explorer, click on **My Documents**. Open your list of documents by clicking on the plus sign by My Documents.

Highlight the file or folder you wish to delete. Go to **File** and from the drop-down menu select **Delete** (or if you prefer, *right* click on the mouse button and click on **Delete**). A **Confirm Folder Delete** message box appears.

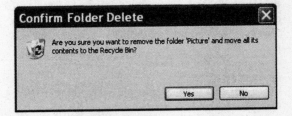

Fig. 15

Action 2

If you have made a mistake and you decide that you wish

to retain the item after all, you can click on **No** and the delete will be cancelled. If you click on **Yes**, the file or folder will be removed and sent to the Recycle Bin.

Section 13:
Deleting Files or Folders from a Floppy Disk

Essential Information

This is a similar process to deleting items from the hard disk but once a file is deleted from a floppy disk it is lost forever – it **does not** go to the Recycle Bin.

Action 1

Open My Computer, click on **Folders** on the toolbar. In the left pane of Explorer, click on the plus sign by **My Computer** to open the folder. Highlight **3½ Floppy** and the files and folders contained on the floppy become listed on the right pane of Explorer. Highlight the item that you wish to delete, and click on **File** on the menu bar (or if you prefer, click on the right mouse button). On the drop-down menu, click on **Delete**. A **Confirm File Delete** message box appears.

Be certain at this stage that you really wish to remove the item, because once deleted it cannot be recalled. It is irrevocably erased. If you wish to keep the document, click on **No**.

If you wish to delete the item, click on **Yes** in the **Confirm Delete File** message box and the item will be erased.

Section 14:
The Recycle Bin

Essential Information
Look at Figure 7 and notice the **Recycle Bin** in the left pane of Explorer. When a file has been deleted from your hard disk it is automatically placed in the Recycle Bin which acts as a receptacle for any unwanted material. It is possible to retrieve material back from the Recycle Bin.

Viewing the contents
Double click on the Recycle Bin icon. The bin's contents will be displayed on the right pane. If the bin is empty then obviously you have not yet deleted any files. If you have deleted a file from the hard disk then it will be listed here.

Restoring a File or Folder
To restore an item from the Recycle Bin back to its original place, click once on the folder or file concerned so that it is highlighted. Now click on **File** on the menu bar, and then click on **Restore** on the drop-down menu (Fig. 16). The file will be returned to its original place from where it was deleted. The word **Restore** will only appear on the menu if you actually have something in the Recycle Bin to restore.

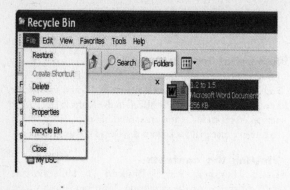

Fig. 16

Deleting a single item

To delete a single item from the bin highlight the file or folder and then click on **File** on the menu bar and click on **Delete** (Fig. 16). It will now be removed completely and cannot be retrieved.

Emptying the Recycle Bin

If you maintain a tidy hard disk and regularly get rid of unwanted material you will eventually find that the Recycle Bin starts to look rather full. To empty the whole bin, click on **File** and then click on **Empty Recycle Bin** (Fig. 17). A message box called **Confirm Multiple File Delete** will ask you if you are sure that you want to delete all the items. Make your decision and then click on Yes or No.

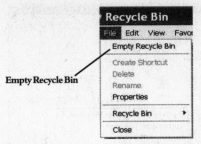

Empty Recycle Bin

Fig. 17

Section 15
My Documents Window: File and Folders Tasks

Essential Information

Many of the tasks above can also be done on the **My Documents** window. The window is divided into two panes. On the left pane are expandable bars which give you access to the various tasks and on the right pane are listed the folders.

Action 1

Open **My Documents** from the Start menu. **Do not** click on the Folders button.

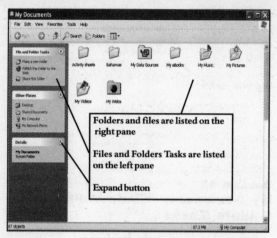

Folders and files are listed on the
right pane

Files and Folders Tasks are listed
on the left pane

Expand button

Fig. 18

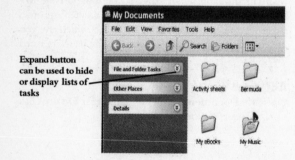

Expand button
can be used to hide
or display lists of
tasks

Fig. 19

Section 16:
Creating a New Folder

Action 1
Under File and Folder Tasks, click on **Make a new folder** (Fig. 20).

Make a new folder

Fig. 20

A new folder appears on the right pane. Delete the words **New folder** (Fig. 21) and type in the name you have chosen for your folder. Press Enter on the keyboard and the new name is saved.

Fig. 21

Section 17:
Moving a Folder

Action 1
Click on the folder that you wish to move, so that it is highlighted. Click on **Move this folder** under File and Folder Tasks and the **Move Items** box appears (Fig. 22). Select the new destination for your folder. Click **Move** and the folder will be moved.

Fig. 22

Section 18:
Copying a Folder

Action 1

Select the folder that you wish to copy by clicking on it.
Under **File and Folder Tasks**, click on **Copy this folder**.
The **Copy Items** box appears (Fig. 23). Select the destination
of the copy of the folder and then click on **Copy**.

Fig. 23

Section 19:
Deleting a Folder

Action 1

Select the folder that you wish to delete. Click on **Delete this folder** under File and Folder Tasks. You will be asked to **Confirm Folder Delete** (Fig. 24). If you are sure you wish to delete the folder click on **Yes** and it will be sent to the Recycle Bin. If you are unsure, click on **No**.

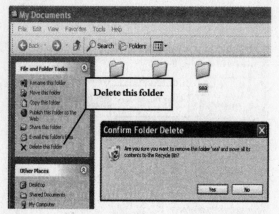

Fig. 24

Chapter Eight:
How to Get Connected to the Internet

Section 1:
The Internet Explained

Essential Information

Put very simply, the Internet is a worldwide system of interconnected computer networks. They are linked via the telephone system and are able to share and exchange information.

The Internet is used for the following:

1. To host the World Wide Web (see *Chapter 9: How to Use the World Wide Web*)
2. To send and receive emails
3. To play games
4. To access newsgroups and information
5. To download software for your computer
6. To access films, television stations, listen to the radio and download music

Section 2:
What sort of Computer do I need to Access the Internet

A computer that has Windows XP will have the capacity to

handle access to the Internet. If you are purchasing a new setup, then try to buy a computer that has a fast processor, a large memory and a modem already installed. This is more important than buying a package with lots of unnecessary software that you will never use.

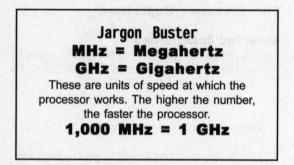

Jargon Buster
MHz = Megahertz
GHz = Gigahertz
These are units of speed at which the processor works. The higher the number, the faster the processor.
1,000 MHz = 1 GHz

The speed of a processor is measured in MHz. Aim for the highest number of MHz that you can afford. 'MB RAM ' is the description of the size of computer memory. Try to get a computer with at least 32 MB RAM and larger if possible. The larger the memory, the faster the computer is able to work and to download material from the Internet.

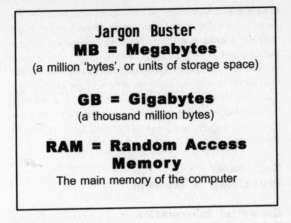

Section 3:
Connecting to the Internet

If you have purchased a new setup you may have the modem and Internet software already installed. All you need to do is plug the telephone cable into the wall socket (and plug in and turn on the computer, of course!). If you do not have a modem installed go to Section 4.

If you feel unable to get your computer set up and connected to the Internet, then it may be a good idea to call in an engineer or your local dealer to do the whole thing for you (but get a quote first).

If you want to set up yourself then start by reading about modems.

Modems

A modem is a device that allows your computer to connect with the telephone system. There are two types internal and external.

The *internal* modem is mounted on a circuit board inside the central processing unit (the 'brain' of the computer). The *external* modem is housed in a small box that sits next to your computer system. If you are unsure whether your computer already has a modem installed it is very easy to check – see Section 5.

Section 4:
Installing a Modem

Essential Information
External Modem

It is possible to install an external modem yourself, as it is just a case of plugging in connections. However this can appear daunting to a beginner. If you have any doubts about your ability it may be a good idea to ask for advice or visual instructions at one of the many large computer stores. Failing this, ask a qualified computer engineer to fit it for you. If you do decide upon an external modem, aim for the fastest that you can afford and one with volume control.

Internal Modem

If your PC does not have an internal modem you can get one installed but this does need to be done by an expert, so ask a qualified engineer to do it for you. Purchase the fastest modem that you can afford.

Section 5:
Detecting a Modem

Essential Information

You can easily check whether a modem has been installed in your computer.

Action 1

Go to the Start menu, click on Control Panel and then click on Phone and Modem Options.

Phone and
Modem Options

Fig. 1

Action 2

The Phone and Modem Options dialogue box opens, click on the Modems tab (Fig. 2). If a modem has been installed, this box will tell you. The make of the modem will also be listed.

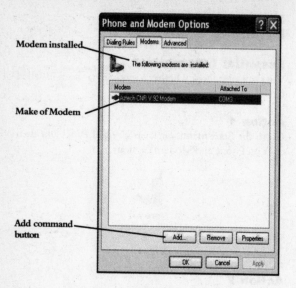

Fig. 2

If there is no modem listed you may still have one, but the computer has to be told to find it. To do this, go to Section 6.

Section 6:
Detecting and Installing a Modem Automatically

The computer needs to search for this new piece of

equipment (hardware) which has been installed. You can either request the system to search for the modem automatically or you can do it manually.

Top Tip
It is a good idea to try to do a manual search
for the modem as it is a good way of
discovering more about how the computer
works.

Action 1

Click once on **Start**, then once on **Control Panel**. Double click on **Phone and Modem Options** icon (Fig. 1) and the **Phone and Modem Options** dialogue box will open (Fig. 2).

Action 2

Single click on the Add button and Add Hardware Wizard Install New Modem will appear (Fig. 3).

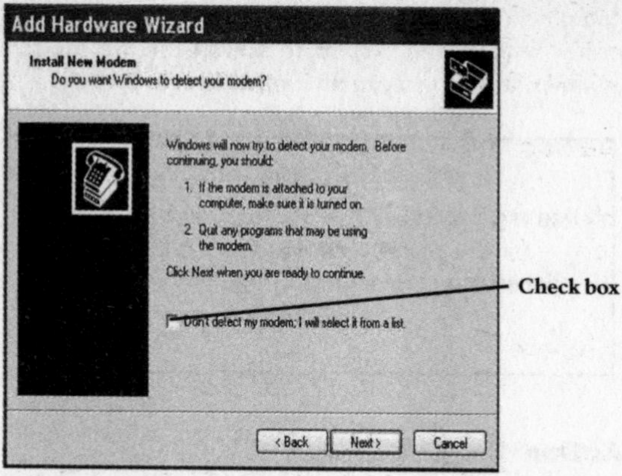

Check box

Fig. 3

Action 3

Remove the tick from the check box **Don't detect my modem; I will select it from a list**. When you remove this tick you will be leaving the computer to automatically detect the modem. Click on **Next>** and the system will commence searching. When the search is completed a box will appear telling you whether or not the modem has been detected. If it has not, then go to Section 7 for a manual search.

Section 7:
Detecting and Installing a Modem Manually

Action 1
Follow the procedure in Section 6 to recall the **Add Hardware Wizard Install New Modems** (Fig. 3) This time make sure that you leave the tick in the check box **Don't detect my modem; I will select it from a list**.

Action 2
Click on **Next>**. The Add Hardware Wizard (Fig. 4) will now ask you to select the model and make of your modem.

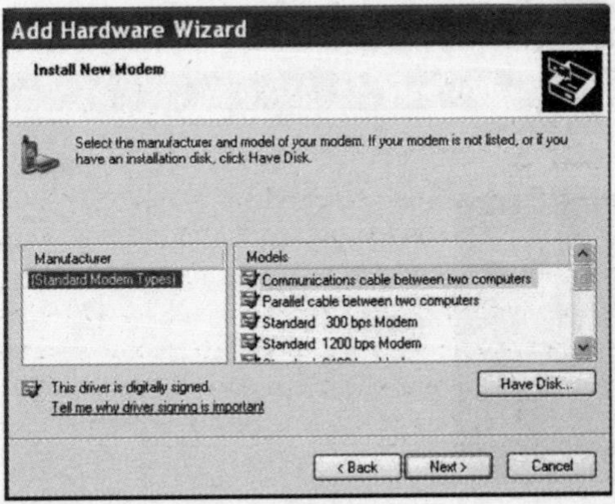

Fig. 4

Click on **Next>**.

Action 3

The next box will ask you to select a communication port (Fig. 5). A communication port is a way of getting information in and out of your computer. It can be an external socket or slot inside the systems unit.

Action 4

If you do not already know which COM port to select, then try COM port 2 (COM 1 is the port often used for the mouse). If a port is already being used by another piece of equipment the computer will tell you that there is a conflict. In this case try one of the other COM ports.

Action 5

Once a COM port has been selected, click on **Next>**.

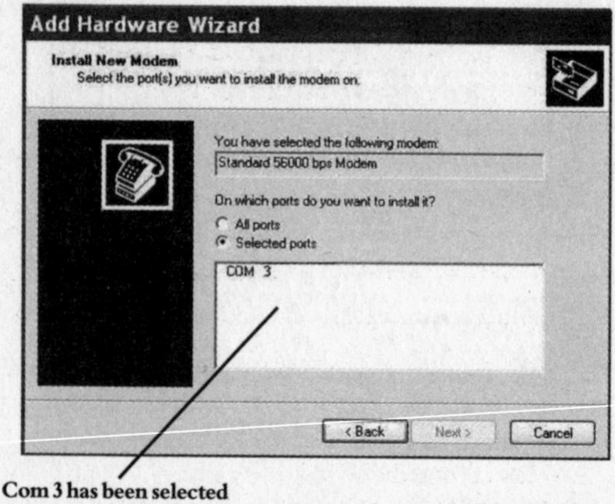

Com 3 has been selected

Fig. 5

The system will then complete its task. Click on **Finish**.

Section 8:
Internet Service Provider

Essential Information

You need to decide which company you are going to use to provide you with your Internet services. There are so many to choose from that it can seem daunting at first but do not be discouraged. The best thing is to first decide what you want from your ISP because they all offer different packages..

Jargon Buster
What is an Internet Access or Service Provider?

An Internet Access Provider (or IAP) is a company which offers access to the Internet and perhaps a few other services. An Internet Service Provider (ISP) also offers access to the Internet but also a fuller and wider range of services.

Look at the following and decide which aspects of the Internet you are interested in using.

1. E-mail only.
2. E-mail and the World Wide Web.
3. Creating and uploading your own web page/site onto the Internet.

4. Online shopping.
5. Do you wish to pay monthly/yearly for your subscription or do you want a free ISP/IAP?
6. Do you want to use the Internet for recreation or do you want to use it for business?.
7. Do you have children and want a family orientated ISP/IAP which has restricted access facility for children?
8. To play games and download software for your PC.
9. To access chat/newsgroups.

Top Tip

To keep phone costs to a minimum, it may be a good idea to access the Internet mainly at weekends and evenings. Check out the phone companies for the latest special Internet access offers.

There are many companies today offering Internet access and a range of services and costs. The most important thing is to take your time, make enquires of each and decide whether what they are offering is actually what you want. As a beginner it is always advisable to keep things as simple as possible and to decide exactly what it is that you want from the Internet. You can then make sure that the company you choose will be delivering the services you want and at the price that you can afford.

Dial-up or Broadband

If you live in an area where Broadband is available, you may wish to consider this as an option. Telephone companies offer a range of packages which combine the cost of Internet and telephone charges delivered via a Broadband connection. Broadband means that the computer is connected to the Internet 24 hours a day, 7 days a week. It's faster at downloading material from the Internet and allows you to use the telephone simultaneously. When you go online there is no need for the computer to dial-up the ISP and so you save time in connecting. However, if you are not going to be a heavy user of the Internet then it may be worth your while to stay with a dial-up connection and a less expensive package from your ISP.

Jargon Buster
Broadband

Broadband requires a cable connection, rather than an overhead telephone line. A special box is fitted indoors to split the signal into telephone and internet signals. It enables large amounts of data to be downloaded quickly and is almost three times faster than a dial up connection.

Jargon Buster
Dial-up

This uses the normal overhead telephone connections to access the Internet which has to be used separately to the telephone. You need to dial up the ISP each time you wish to browse the web.

UK Libraries and Internet Cafés

The Internet is currently being installed in all UK libraries. Phone to check which libraries in your area have so far been connected. Access is for all and is not limited to special groups such as students. There will probably be a small charge. There should be help available from library staff.

Internet or **Cyber Cafes** are also a good way of gaining an introduction to the Internet. They are very relaxed and usually inexpensive places where you can also buy tea, coffee and other snacks. There is normally a set charge and you only pay for the amount of time spent online. You can explore the web or send e-mails and if you get stuck or need help there is usually someone available. Most places have a minimum period charge of half an hour. Some of the larger Internet cafes now offer short courses for beginners.

Section 9:
Contacting an IAP/ISP

Essential Information

Once you have decided what you want from an IAP/ISP, and chosen a few likely companies, phone them up and tackle them with the following list of questions and requests, (and anything else that you may have thought of!)

1. Ask for an information pack.
2. Look for a company, which provides you with a CD-ROM that is pre-configured for easy installation. This means less worry for you.
3. Make sure the company that you choose uses the **POP 3** mail system.

Jargon Buster
What is a POP Account?
(Post Office Protocol)

POP accounts are local area telephone numbers that your ISP works through enabling you to e-mail and connect to the Web at local telephone rates.

---

4. Do they provide a telephone helpline and what times are they available? Some work 'early to late', others 24 hours and some only during the week and not at weekends. Make sure a helpline is

available for when you are going to be using the
Internet.

5. Is the helpline manned by people who are willing and able to talk you through problems?

6. Is the helpline free? If not how much do they charge. Consider for example that a charge of 50p per minute can soon mount up if you require a lot of support.

7. What is their yearly fee or, if you prefer, the monthly subscription?

8. Do not purchase an ISP/IAP which also charges you to go online. The most you should pay is your normal telephone rate.

9. Find out what other services they offer. Decide if you really want them. Don't buy an ISP/IAP with bells and whistles on, if all you want to do is send an e-mail.

Top Tip
Aim for a server who offers you a POP 3 account because this will also enable you to access your e-mail from a variety of sources and not just via your ISP. This will give you the flexibility to read your e-mail at work, home, library or wherever you have access to a computer.

Telephone Charges
Essential Information

Remember that the only way that you can connect to the Internet to send e-mails or surf the web is to use the telephone system. Every time you go online your computer modem is making a phone call and you are paying for it.

Action 1
Keeping Bills in Check

1. Make sure your ISP uses only local phone numbers. (POP 3)
2. Time the length of time you spend on the Internet – and at the end of that period come off line.
3. Work offline whenever the opportunity allows.
4. Don't go on line during peak periods.
5. Send your ISP phone number to any of the discount schemes offered by your phone company.
6. Look around for special offers: some companies provide free access to the internet if you pay a monthly subscription.

Section 10:
Signing up

Essential Information

Once you have decided upon an ISP, they will send you the necessary software on a CD-ROM.

Action 1

Every service provider will of course have different instructions, but first of all you will need to load the CD-ROM.

Action 2

You will need a password and a user name. Take some time to think of an unusual word – don't just spell your name backwards! This password should be kept secret. It is your security against other people using your ISP and your phone or even accessing your information.

Action 3

Before you begin the setup procedure have the following ready.

1. The reference number on the software package.
2. If you haven't signed up and paid already by post, you will need to do so online so have your credit/debit card ready.
3. The ISP will give you a user name and password in order to commence, but once you are online change these to your selection.

Action 4

On the screen will appear a series of instructions – just follow them and your setup will be completed automatically. Remember if you have problems this is where that helpline is really invaluable.

Top Tip
If you make a mistake whilst trying to set-up don't worry just cancel or exit the procedure and start again.

At the end of the procedure you will have the choice of going on line immediately or later.

Section 11:
Logging On

Essential Information
Once your ISP program has been loaded onto your system all the hard work has been completed In future, it will be a simple process to get online.

Action 1
Open your Internet Explorer program by double - clicking on the icon that was automatically created and placed on your desktop, and the first connect box will appear automatically.

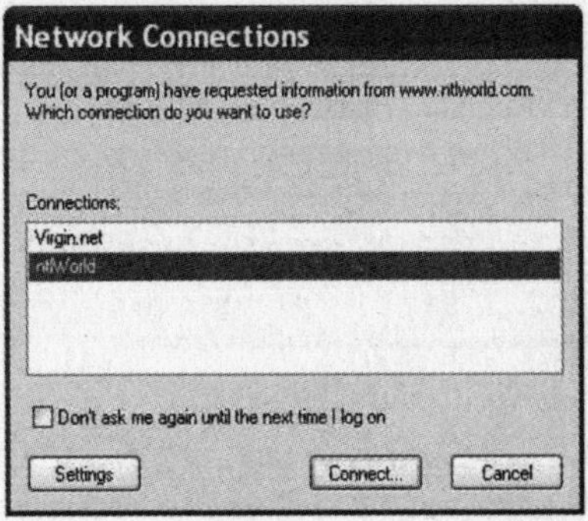

Network Connections

You (or a program) have requested information from www.ntlworld.com. Which connection do you want to use?

Connections:

Virgin.net

ntlworld

☐ Don't ask me again until the next time I log on

[Settings]   [Connect...]   [Cancel]

Fig. 6

Click on **connect** and a second box will appear as in Fig. 8. Alternatively click on Start, Connect To and click on whichever Network Connection is listed (Fig. 7).

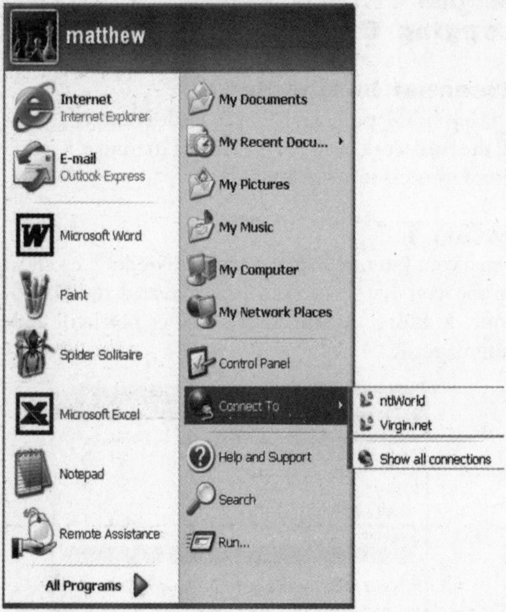

Fig. 7

A connect box will appear on the screen (Fig. 8). Enter your password and then click on Dial.

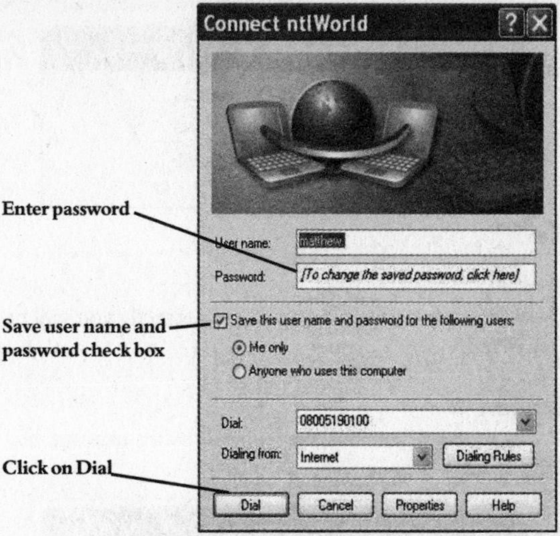

Enter password

Save user name and password check box

Click on Dial

Fig. 8

Top Tip
Once you are confident about typing in the
correct password you can save time later by
clicking in the check box of the 'Save the user
name and password'.

A message box will inform you that the modem is dialling
your ISP (Fig. 9).

> **Connecting ntlWorld...**
>
> Dialing 0800519010 0...
>
> [Cancel]

Fig. 9

If your have typed in your password correctly you will be connected.

Action 2

If you have made a mistake, the following message box will appear.

Fig. 10

Follow the advice in the message box, as you may have made a mistake when typing your password. You can either click on redial or start again and re-enter your password.

Section 12:
Disconnecting

Action 1

Look at the bottom right-hand corner of your monitor.
Adjacent to the digital time you will see two blue computers,
one behind the other. This is the connection icon (Fig. 11).
If it is not visible go to Section 13.

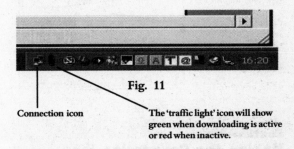

Fig. 11

Connection icon   The 'traffic light' icon will show
green when downloading is active
or red when inactive.

Double click on this icon and a **Status** message box will
open (Fig. 12). Click on the button that says **Disconnect**
and the computer closes down the telephone link to the
Internet. The connection icon on the taskbar then
disappears.

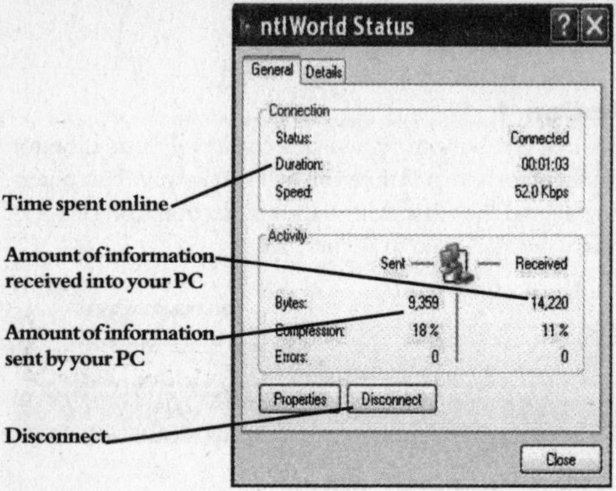

Time spent online

Amount of information
received into your PC

Amount of information
sent by your PC

Disconnect

Fig. 12

Section 13:
Making the Connection Icon
Visible

Essential Information
You may need to take action to make the connection icon
visible on the taskbar.

Action 1
Go to **Start**, click on **Control Panel**. Click on **Network
Connections** (Fig. 13).

Network
Connections

Fig. 13

The **Network Connection** window opens (Fig. 14). Right click on the connection icon and from the drop-down list select Properties.

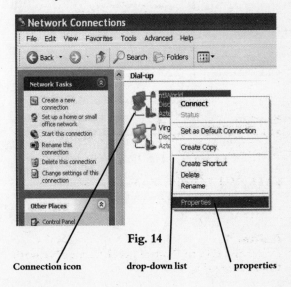

Fig. 14

Connection icon   drop-down list   properties

The **Properties** dialogue box opens (Fig. 15). Make sure the **General** tab is selected. Click on the check box by the words **Show icon in notification area when connected**. There should now be a tick in the check box.

Click on check box

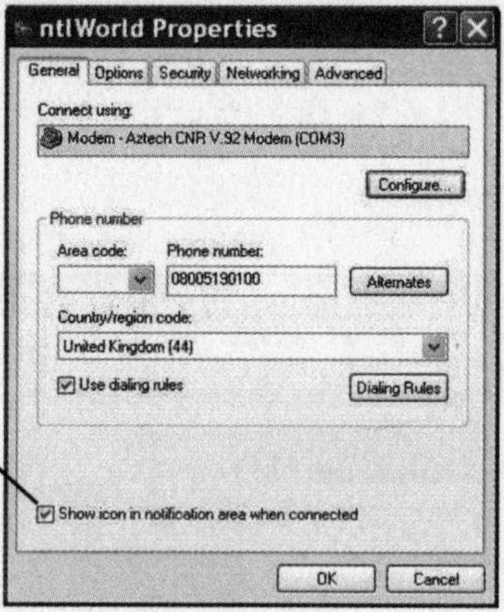

Fig. 15

Click on **OK**.

Chapter Nine:
How to Use the World Wide Web

Section 1:
What is the World Wide Web?

Essential Information
The World Wide Web is a phenomenon hosted by the Internet. A web site, like a book, is made up of individual pages. There are millions of web sites on the Internet and no one is quite sure how many millions of pages there are. Many more are added each day.

Information on the Web
Information on the Web comes from many sources; from people and organisations that wish to inform and share knowledge about their own areas of expertise. The list is huge and includes governments, research establishments, universities, schools, businesses, pressure groups, TV companies, charities, fan clubs, retail outlets, travel and entertainment guides.

The web is truly international, so information can be sourced directly from the company or country in which you are interested. There is a large amount of excellent material out there but, just like any library, not everything is of high quality.

Anyone who has access to a domain (web site) can create their own web page and then upload it onto the Internet, where it can be accessed by others. One of the skills you will develop when using the Internet is how to sift out what you want from the enormous amount of information stored on the Web.

What are Web Browsers?

In order to view the Web you need a program called a web browser. Microsoft **Internet Explorer** is a web browser which, if you have XP, will already be on your PC. You can install others if you wish by downloading them from the Internet or from your ISP.

Section 2:
Getting onto the Web

Action 1

1. Go to Start, and click on **Internet Explorer**.
2. Alternatively if you have a shortcut to Internet Explorer on the desktop, double - click on it and it will lead you straight into the program.

Action 2

Once you have launched Internet Explorer (or any other web browser) it will invite you to connect to the Internet. (Read *Chapter 8: How to Get Connected to the Internet*). Before you go online, take some time to familiarise yourself with the various functions of your web browser.

Section 3:
Internet Explorer

Essential Information

At the top of the Internet Explorer window is a menu bar, a standard buttons bar and the address bar. These tools allow you to navigate the web and to manage material. Take a little time to familiarise yourself with the following before you go online:

Fig. 1

The most useful tools on the Standard button bar are:

Back and Forward

Fig. 2

Fig. 3

Once pages have been downloaded onto your computer it is possible to use the buttons at the top of the screen to go back and forward between pages that you have already visited. This is often quicker that using the links within the web site.

Stop

Fig. 4

This button stops a page from downloading onto the screen. It's useful if you have dialled in the wrong web address and wish to stop the delivery of a page, or if you do not like the look of a site as it initially comes onto the screen. By using this button you can save yourself time and, of course, money if you are paying for the Internet call.

Refresh

Fig. 5

This button allows you to reload an existing page onto the screen if it doesn't appear properly the first time. It gives the system a chance to locate all the information and place it in the correct order. It also updates a previously saved page.

Print

Fig. 6

This button allows you to print a copy of a page from a site.

Top Tip
Printing a web page
Be aware that a page on a web site can be a
lot longer than a conventional A4 sheet of
paper. You could end up printing reams of
paper for one tiny piece of information.

Favorites

Fig. 7

This button allows you to record the web address of a site as
you browse the Web. The web address enters the computer
memory and you are then able to recall it at a later date and
log onto the site directly. It is a very convenient way of
keeping a list of sites that you like and may wish to revisit.
It is also much easier than writing down the web address
manually.

The Menu Bar: File and Edit

The **File** drop-down menu (Fig. 8) allows you to save and print a page. And the **Edit** drop-down menu (Fig. 9) enables you to cut, copy and paste items. To use any of these tools follow the same procedure as for a Word document.

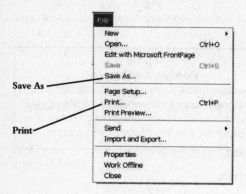

Fig. 8

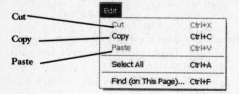

Fig. 9

The Address Bar

This is where you type in the web address of a web site.

Address | http://www.hdra.org.uk/   ▼ | → Go

Fig. 10

In Figure 10 the web address of the HDRA is shown in the address bar. Once you have typed in the address click on the **Go** button or press Enter on the keyboard and the web site will be located.

Section 4:
Web Addresses and the Address Bar

Essential Information

Every web site has its own web address and each page within that site also has its own address. These addresses are a unique identification mechanism, a bit like DNA or fingerprints. There are millions of pages that are contained within the Internet and they all need to carry some special reference, in order that they can be identified and loaded onto your screen. These references are called Uniform Resource Locators or **URL**s. They are typed into the address bar of Internet Explorer (Fig. 10).

Action 1

Look at this example of a web address. It's for the Imperial War Museum in London. Notice what the abbreviations stand for but don't be intimidated by them! You do not need to know what these things mean, just concentrate on keeping the web address accurate.

http://www.iwm.org.uk/index

http://	Hypertext Transfer Protocol
www	World Wide Web
iwm	Organisation name i.e. Imperial War Museum
org	Type of organisation i.e. co., com., org., gov.)
uk	Country
/index	Page

Action 2

Notice the dots, colons and forward slashes. These are very important and must not be left out. There are also no spaces in the address.

Top Tip

If a web address will not work, check that:
1. You have not left out any dots or slashes.
2. You have not added any dots, slashes or spaces
3. You have not omitted a letter, i.e. og instead of org

Action 3

Type a web address into the text box on the address bar. Press **Enter** or click on the **Go** button. The Internet Service Provider then searches the whole World Wide Web (WWW) to find the correct address that you are seeking.

Once the address had been located, the web site will start to download. The first page of a web site that usually arrives onto the screen is the site's home page or a welcome page.

Section 5:
Layout of the Web Page

Essential Information

Each web page has a **home page.** It's the home page that carries the web address, which is registered with an ISP (Internet Service Provider) and usually with an international search engine. Imagine the home page as a combination of a front cover of a book and the contents page; enticing and encouraging you to explore further and trying to keep you from disappearing onto another site. A page can contain text, graphics and pictures. It can be very simple or very detailed.

On the home page you will find various links that will lead you through the pages of the web site. You may have a further contents list or what is known as an image map, if the site is a large one.

Action 1

Look at the HDRA home page in Figure 11. This page is representative of many web sites which will also have similar features.

HDRA web address

HDRA Search box to search the
HDRA site quickly for a specific
item

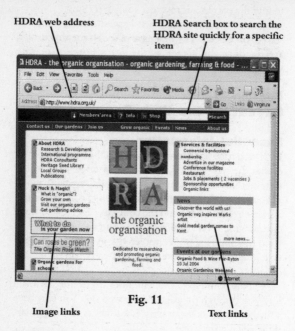

Fig. 11

Image links

Text links

Action 2

By clicking on the image link **What to do in your garden
now**, a new page is downloaded (Fig. 12). The web address
of the new page is the same as the home page but with the
addition of **/todo_now/index.php** which identifies it.

How to Use the World Wide Web

A page within a web site carries the main web site address (or URL) plus its own page identification

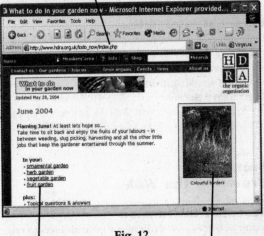

Fig. 12

Further text links take you into more pages of the web site

Picture link

Jargon Buster
HTML
Hypertext Mark-up Language
This is the language in which most web pages are written.

Section 6:
How to Spot a Link

Essential Information

Links can exist as text, pictures or graphics. Textual links are usually in blue and are underlined. If you are not sure whether some text is a link, just move the pointer onto it and if the arrow turns into a small hand with a pointed finger then it is a link.

To activate the link, wait until the pointer turns into a hand, click and you will be taken to the linked page.

Section 7:
Browsing the Web

Essential Information

Many web sites now dedicate a page with links to other sites that have similar interests. If you click on these links you will be taken off the original site and on to a different site. Sometimes these can lead to dead ends with either no further links or subjects that don't interest you. Use the **Back** button (Figs. 1 and 2) to return to the previous site and then head off in a different direction. Add interesting sites to your list of favourites as you go; it is easier than writing them down or retracing your steps. (More on the Favorites function in Section 8.)

The phrase 'Browsing the Web' may be an expression already familiar to you. It simply means following links from one site to another to see what is available, like browsing along a set of books in the library. Sometimes you may stop to read an item and other times pass on by.

Section 8:
Your Favorites List

Essential Information
The Favorites function is very useful in allowing you to keep a record of web sites visited. By clicking on an entry in the Favorites list the web address is entered straight into the address bar of Internet Explorer.

Action 1
Click on the **Favorites** button and the browser window splits into two.

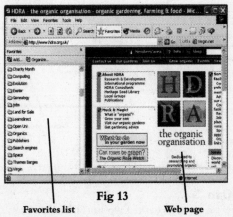

Fig 13

Favorites list   Web page

Web sites that have been previously added to the list of favourite sites are listed in alphabetical order. By clicking again on Favorites so that the button is no longer depressed, the split screen disappears and there is more space to view a web page.

Action 2

To add a page to Favorites while you are online, click on **Add** on the Favorites bar. The **Add Favorite** box is displayed (Fig. 14). The names of the page that you are currently viewing will appear automatically in the text box.

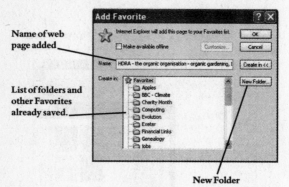

Name of web page added

List of folders and other Favorites already saved.

New Folder

Fig. 14

Click **OK** and the page will be added to your list of Favorites.

Action 3

To revisit a site, go to the Favorites button, click once, the screen will split and the web pages will be listed in the left-hand panel, either as single items or in a folder. To open a folder just click on it and the single items will be displayed. Click on the one that you wish to revisit.

Section 9:
Creating a New Folder for Your Favorites

Action 1
Click on the **Favorites** button and click on **Add** and the **Add Favorite** box appears (Fig. 14).

Action 2
Click on the **New Folder** button (Fig. 14). The **Create New Folder** box is displayed (Fig. 15). Type in the name that you have chosen for the new folder. Click **OK.**

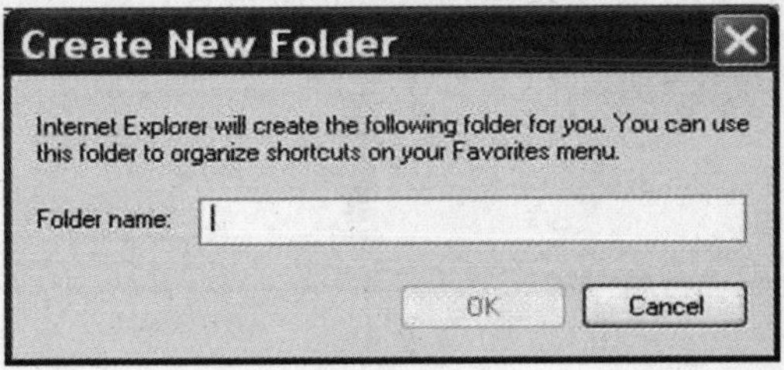

Create New Folder   ✕

Internet Explorer will create the following folder for you. You can use this folder to organize shortcuts on your Favorites menu.

Folder name: [   ]

                                    OK   Cancel

Fig. 15

Section 10:
Renaming, Moving and Deleting Folders

Renaming

Click on the **Favorites** button and click on **Organize**. **Organize Favourites** is displayed (Fig. 16). Highlight the folder concerned and then click on **Rename**. You will then be able type in a new name. Press **Enter** on the keyboard and the new name is saved.

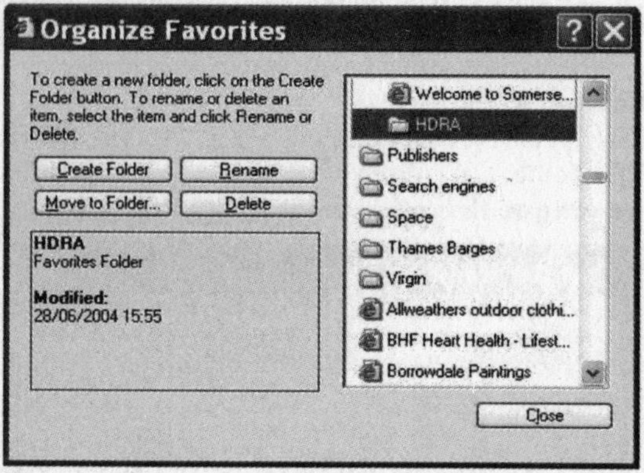

Fig. 16

Moving a Folder

To move an item into a folder, open **Organize Favorites** (Fig. 16) and highlight the folder to be moved. Click on **Move to Folder** (Fig. 16) and **Browse for Folder** is displayed (Fig. 17).

Action 3

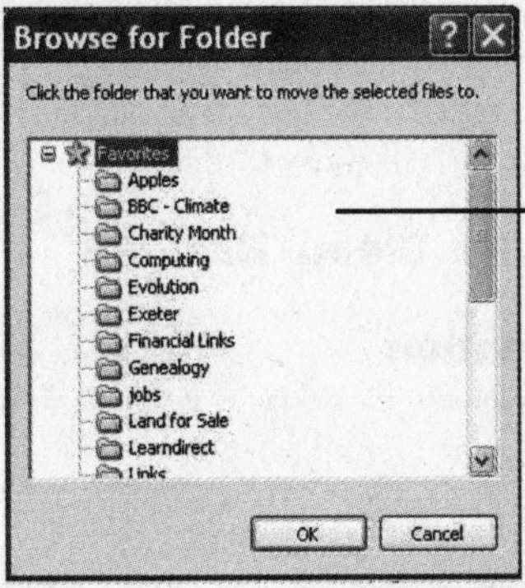

Click on the folder that you want to move the file into.

Fig. 17

Then click on **OK** and the folder will be moved into its new position.

Deleting a Folder

Eventually you will wish to remove items from your Favorites list. Open **Organize Favorites** (Fig. 16). Select the item to be deleted. Click on the **Delete** button. A message box will ask you if you wish to send the item to the Recycle Bin. Click on **Yes** to dump or **No** if you've changed your mind.

Top Tip
Delete unwanted items regularly and
organise the rest into logically named folders.
This will save you time in searching for a
specific page which you once visited.

Section 11:
Favorites on the Menu Bar.

Essential Information
You can also add and organize Favorites by going to **File**
on the menu bar.

Action 1
Click on the word **Favorites** on the menu and a
drop - down menu will appear (Fig. 18).

Fig. 18

Action 2
Click on either **Add to Favorites** or **Organize Favorites**
and follow the same procedure for each as shown in the
sections above.

Section 12:
Searching the Web

Essential Information

If you wish to search for a specific topic you will need to use the web search tools to help you sift through the vast array of information available. These search tools are called search engines and web directories.

Search Engines...

are enormous indexes of web pages built automatically by a computer program. A search engine combs the Web for information, searching for compatibility with certain keywords that you have provided (Fig. 19).

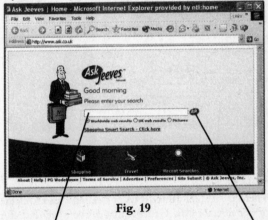

Fig. 19

Click in text box and then type in subject or keywords.   Click on Ask.

Web Directories...

are organised, logical lists based on a variety of chosen categories. Each category is subdivided into further groups, which are again subdivided. It is an efficient way of progressively narrowing down your search and of achieving positive and relevant results. They are designed to be user-friendly and also provide a keyword search facility.

Search text box

Fig. 20

Click on a topic and a range of relevant subjects will be downloaded.

There are generally three ways of locating a search engine or web directory: direct access, through your web browser or through your ISP.

Direct Access

In the text box on the address bar, type in the web address of the search tool. Press return on your keyboard. The home page should begin to download.

There are a number of companies who offer these facilities for free. Here is a list of some of them:

Ask Jeeves	www.ask.co.uk
AltaVista	www.altavista.com
Google	www.google.co.uk
Hot Bot	www.hotbot.com
directory.co.uk	www.directory.co.uk
Uk Plus	www.ukplus.co.uk
Excite	www.excite.com
Lycos	www.lycos.com
Go	www.go.com

Through Your Web Browser

Internet Explorer has a search button on the web browser toolbar (Fig. 21). To get to the search list on Internet Explorer, click on the **Search** button and on the left side of the window the search companion will be listed.

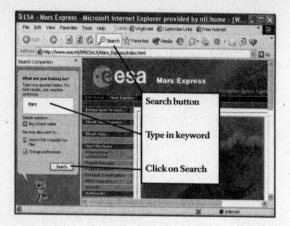

Fig. 21

Through Your ISP

There may be a search button on the home page of your ISP. Click on it and a selection of search tools will be downloaded.

Section 13:
Single Country Search

Essential Information

Most search engines are international in their scope. If you wish, you can limit information that you access to just one country.

Action 1

Look at Figure 22. This shows the home page of the Google Search engine.

It is representative of many other search tools in allowing you to select a particular country. By clicking on **UK**, the Google will limit its search to sites deemed more relevant for a UK audience.

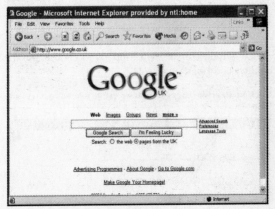

Fig. 22

Action 2

Scroll to the bottom of Google's home page, and there a link called **Language Tools**.

Language Tools

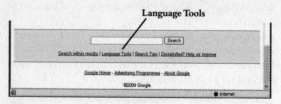

Fig. 23

A new window opens with options to choose another country and language (Fig 24).

Click on the arrows to get drop-down lists to select a country and a language

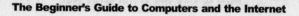

Fig. 24

Section 14:
Searching Using Keywords

Essential Information

Most search engines and many directories will provide a keyword search facility. When you type in your keywords the search engine will attempt to match them to words in a web site title or in the contents of the first page. Very often a single word will find what you want. If you need to use more than one word, always type them in the descending order of importance.

Action 1

Look at Figure 25. The word **volcanoes** was typed into the **Search** text box and then the search button was single clicked. A huge number of results were listed – 73,900!

Fig. 25

Action 2

To reduce the number of web sites on the results list you may need to narrow your search. This can be done by typing in keywords into the search text box in descending order of importance. For example 'volcano, etna, eruptions, 20th century' (don't forget a comma after each keyword) produced a list of 75 sites, which is much more manageable.

Volcano, etna, eruptions, 20th century

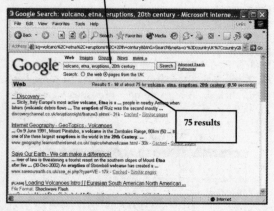

Fig. 26

Those sites that have the best matches to the keywords are always listed first. So the first 10–20 will be the most relevant.

Section 15:
Searching for a Specific Phrase

Essential Information

It is possible to find a site using a specific phrase. Type the phrase into the keyword box on the search tool that you have chosen and be sure to place it in quotation marks.

Action 1

Look at Figure 27. In the **search** text box is **I have a dream**. The search button was clicked and Google found a number of relevant sites, including one about Martin Luther King, who originated the phrase.

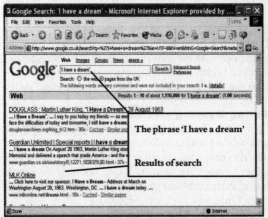

Fig. 27

Section 16:
Safety and Security on the Internet

Internet Service Providers
More ISPs are now aware of the need for filtering information to make it acceptable for family viewing and are seeking to provide customers with integral programs that take care of the supervision of web sites. If you want such a service, remember to ask before you sign up.

Software Programs Available
There are software programs available independently of your ISP. These programs work behind the scenes scanning all pages for unacceptable content.

Go Online to get More Information.
Net Nanny: http://www.net-nanny-software.com
Cyber Sitter (Offers free download): http://www.cybersitter.com
Parental Control Software: www.pctabletalk.com
I am Big Brother software: www.software4parents.com

Online Banking and Online Shopping
Great strides have been made in security over the Internet and online banking and shopping are now a fact of life. The encoding devices used are of the highest quality in the effort to maintain security. However only ever make financial transactions or give personal information on secure sites. Once you click on a shopping/banking page you should be told that you are about to enter a secure site (Fig. 28).

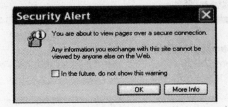

Fig. 28

If you are not sure whether or not the site is secure, look for the padlock at the bottom of the window on Internet Explorer.

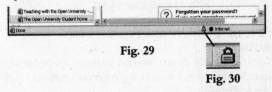

Fig. 29

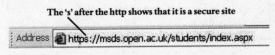

Fig. 30

Another way of identifying a secure site is to look at the http:// part of the web address. If the site is secure it becomes https:// (Fig. 31).

The 's' after the http shows that it is a secure site

Address https://msds.open.ac.uk/students/index.aspx

Fig. 31

305

Section 17:
Internet Privacy Levels

Essential Information

It is possible to control the use of cookies stored on your computer by Internet sites.

Jargon Buster
Cookies

Temporary internet files that are generated when you visit a web site. Contains very basic information about your visit.

Action 1

Click on **Tools** on the Internet Explorer menu bar and from the drop-down menu select **Internet Options**. Click on the **Privacy** tab (Fig. 32).

Top Tip

If you block all cookies you may not be able to access some web sites.

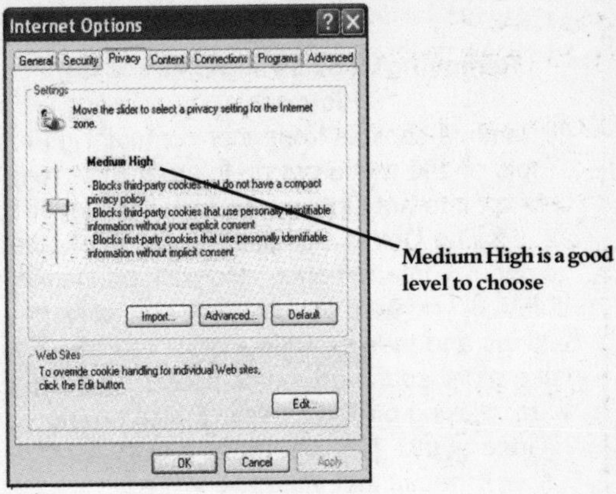

Medium High is a good level to choose

Fig. 32

Action 2

Move the slider either up or down to select a level. Click on **Apply** and then **OK**.

Top Tip
Removing Cookies and Clearing the
History List
To remove cookies from your computer go to
Tools on the menu bar on Internet Explorer,
click on Internet Options, click on the General
tab, click on Delete Cookies. To get rid of other
temporary internet files, also click on Delete
Files. (If you wish to view them first, click on
Settings and then on View Files). You can also
make more space on the computer hard **drive**
by clicking on Clear History, also on the
General tab. This clears the history list of
pages that you have visited.

Section 18:
Firewall Protection

Essential Information

Windows Firewall protects your computer from invasion
by outsiders when you are on the Internet. It is a barrier
between hackers and your hard drive. It is very simple to
turn on or off and adds another level of security to your
PC.

Action 1

Click on **Tools** on the Internet Explorer menu bar and

from the drop-down menu select **Internet Options**. Click on the **Connections** tab. Click on **Settings** (Fig. 33) and then on **Properties** (Fig. 34).

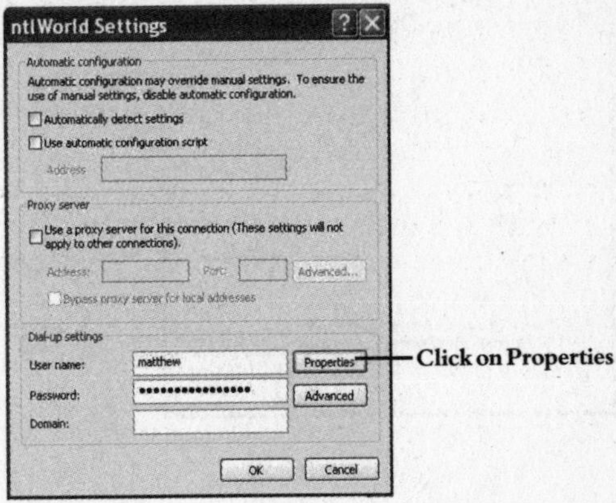

Fig. 33

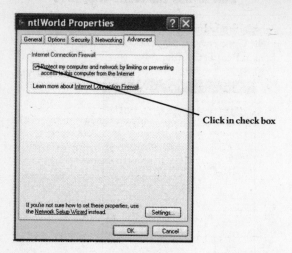

Click in check box

Fig. 34

Action 2
Click in the check box to activate the firewall. Click **OK**.

Help on Internet Explorer
Microsoft Internet Explorer offers advice on safety and security. To find out more, open up Internet Explorer and click on the **Help** button (Fig. 35).

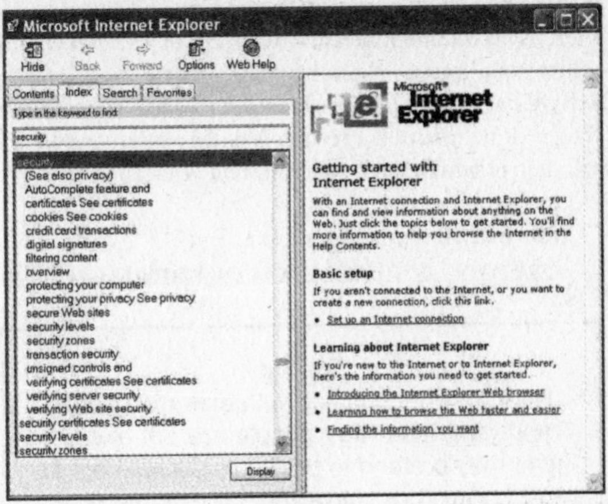

Fig. 35

Some subjects that you may wish to check out are:

1. Filtering content
2. Protecting your computer
3. Protecting your privacy
4. Transaction security

Section 19:
Internet Chat

Essential Information

Chat rooms are places where like-minded people can

exchange news and views on the Internet. Chat rooms are often listed on the homepage of an ISP or a search engine or directory. You can also access networks that host Internet Relay Chat (IRC). IRC enables you to 'chat' in real time. This is done through a server. Whichever server you use will dictate which IRC network that you can join.

Information is available online. Try:
http://www.bbc.co.uk/webwise/guides/mirc/mircl.shtml

Top Tip
Treat Internet chatting with extreme caution and remember that people are not always who they pretend to be. It is advisable not to let children or vulnerable people use chat rooms or have access to IRC.

TV Chat

Many TV companies now attach an online chat service to some of their popular programs. These allow you to participate in interviewing experts and personalities about subjects broadcast on TV programs.

Section 20:
A Selection of Web Sites

Essential Information

There are literally millions of web sites on the Internet. Here are a few to start you off on your Internet odyssey! All of them begin with http:// so make sure that this is present in the web browser address bar before you type in the rest of the address. There are a few addresses included which do not contain www – this is not a printing mistake – the letters are simply not required for that particular address. For example: http://gollum.usask.ca/tolkien/index.html. Happy browsing!

Sports
Tennis
www.wimbleledon.com
Football
www.soccernet.com
Golf
www.golf.com
Rugby
www.rfl.uk.com
Cricket
www.cricinfo.com

Museums and Military History
Imperial War Museum
www.iwm.org.uk
Commonwealth War Grave
www.cwgc.org/cwgcinternet/search.aspx

National Army Museum
www.national-army-museum.ac.uk/index.html
Western Front
www.westernfront.co.uk
Battle of Britain
www.raf.mod.uk/bob1940/
British Library
www.bl.uk
Victoria and Albert Museum
www.vam.ac.uk
Bodlian Library
www.bodley.ox.ac.uk
British Museum
www.british-museum.ac.uk
Museum of London
www.museumoflondon.org
National Maritime Museum
www.port.nmm.ac.uk

Government and Royalty
The British Monarchy
www.royal.gov.uk
The Royal Collection
www.the-royal-collection.org.uk
Prince of Wales
www.princeofwales.gov.uk
Royal genealogical data
www.dcs.hull.ac.uk/public/genealogy/GEDCOM.html
10, Downing Street
www.number-10.gov.uk

House of Commons
www.parliament.uk/commons/hsecom.htm
European Parliament
www.europarl.org.uk
Government Information
www.direct.gov.uk/Homepage/fs/en
The White House
www.whitehouse.gov/

Travel
Travellersweb
www.travellersweb.ws/
Railtrack
www.railtrack.com
Cheapflights.com
www.cheapflights.com

Books
Amazon Books
www.amazon.co.uk
The Children's Bookshop
www.childrensbookshop.com
J.R.R.Tolkein
http://gollum.usask.ca/tolkien/index.html
Terry Pratchet
www.us.lspace.org/
Harry Potter sites
www.harrypotter.warnerbros.co.uk
On-line Encyclopaedia
www.britannica.com

Newspapers

British Library
www.bl.uk/catalogues/newspapers/welcome.asp
Electronic Telegraph
www.telegraph.co.uk
Financial Times
www.ft.com
The Guardian
www.guardian.co.uk
The Times
www.the-times.co.uk

Genealogy and History

Doomsday Book Online
www.domesdaybook.co.uk
English Heritage
www.english-heritage.org.uk
Historic Scotland
www.historic-scotland.gov.uk
Borthwick Institute of Historic Research
www.york.ac.uk/inst/bihr
Society of Genealogy
www.sog.org.uk
Genuki
www.genuki.org.uk/big
Cyndis List of Genealogy sites on the Internet
www.cyndislist.com
Institute of Genealogy and Historic Studies
www.ihgs.ac.uk
General Record Office for Scotland
www.gro-scotland.gov.uk

Public Record Office
www.pro.gov.uk
National Archives
www.nationalarchives.gov.uk

Science
The Science Museum
www.sciencemuseum.org.uk
The Smithsonian Institute
www.si.edu
The Met Office
www.met-office.gov.uk
European Space Agency
www.esa.int/export/esaCP/index.html
British Space Agency
www.bnsc.gov.uk
Nasa
www.nasa.gov

Environment
Royal Horticultural Society
www.rhs.org.uk
The National Trust
www.nationaltrust.org.uk
Greenpeace
www.greenpeace.org.uk
Eden Project
www.edenproject.com
Friends of the Earth
www.foe.co.uk

H.D.R.A
www.hdra.org.uk
The Forestry Commission
www.forestry.gov.uk
The Wildlife Trust
www.wildlifetrust.org.uk/
RSPB
www.rspb.org.uk/noflash.html
The British Mammal Society
www.abdn.ac.uk/mammal/
RSPCA
www.rspca.org.uk

Arts and Entertainment
National Gallery
www.nationalgallery.org.uk
Tate Gallery
www.tate.org.uk
Internet Movies Database
www.imdb.com
British Film Institute
www.bfi.co.uk
BBC
www.bbc.co.uk
Channel 4
www.channel4.com
ITV
www.itv.co.uk
Sky
www.sky.com

Chapter Ten:
How to Use E-mail and Outlook Express

Section 1:
Your E-mail Program

Essential Information

E-mail is short for 'electronic mail'. It allows information to be sent anywhere in the world from one computer to another via the telephone system. It is particularly useful for contacting people abroad or sending short messages.

Jargon Buster
Snail Mail

The traditional postal service has been dubbed 'snail mail' because of its relative slowness of delivery in comparison with the speed of e-mail.

There are various e-mail programs to choose from. The e-mail program **Outlook Express** is an integral part of Windows XP and is the one covered by this book. You can however download other email programs from the Internet; you do not have to stick to just one system.

Here are three examples of other e-mail programs:

Eudora Light – This free e-mail program can be downloaded from **http://www.eudora.com**

Netscape – A free e-mail program that can be downloaded from **http://www.eudora.com**

Hotmail – a very popular e-mail service. Information is available from **http://www.hotmail.com**

If you are not yet on the Internet then you will need to select an Internet Service Provider (ISP which will include an e-mail facility with the package that you choose. If you skipped over the Internet section, go back and read it, as the information is relevant to e-mailing).

As well as an Internet Service Provider you will also need an internal or external modem connected to your computer (see Chapter 8) and a 'plug in' or broadband telephone connection

Section 2:
E-mail Addresses

Essential Information

To send and receive e-mails you must have an e-mail address – just as you need a home address to receive traditional post. Each e-mail address is unique, rather like your home address. If you do not want to use your full name on the address you can always choose a nickname.

Action 1

Look at the sample e-mail address below. Notice that the address is all in lower case letters and includes dots (or full stops) which are very important. If you leave them out the e-mail address will not operate. Also there are no spaces between words and if you put them in, the e-mail address will not operate.

The e-mail address contains certain parts:

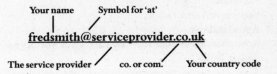

Your name   Symbol for 'at'

fredsmith@serviceprovider.co.uk

The service provider   co. or com.   Your country code

Action 2

Look at the e-mail address below. Outside America, a code is used to represent a country, so if Fred Smith lived in Australia, his e-mail code might be:

fredsmith@serviceprovider.co.au

Section 3:
Setting Up Outlook Express

Essential Information

Outlook Express will need to be set up (configured). Before you start, make sure that you have the following information ready:

> User name
> Password
> Your chosen email name
> E-mail address
> Any other details your ISP may have given you about your account.

Configuring or setting up the e-mail is done by a **Wizard**, which will request certain details from you then make the mail connection. The Wizard will lead you through the procedure.

Action 1

Follow the instructions and if you are unsure about some of the checkboxes then leave them alone and the computer will set their defaults. What you must fill in are details about your e-mail account and your service provider.

Action 2

Any problems? This is where your ISP telephone helpline comes in handy. Tell them your difficulty and ask them to take you through the procedure from the beginning. It really does save a lot of hassle! If you really are stuck ask a qualified engineer to assist – you can find them in the telephone book (get a quote first). Once the settings have been made (i.e. configured) you will be ready to send and receive your e-mail messages.

Section 4:
Opening Outlook Express

Action 1
Double click on the Outlook Express icon your desktop.

Outlook
Express (2)

Fig. 1

Or click on **Start** and then click on **Email Outlook Express.**

Fig. 2

Action 2

You will now be asked to connect to the Internet. The connection procedure is the same for e-mailing as it is for the Internet. If you have forgotten how to do this refer back to Chapter 8.

Section 5:
The E-mail Window

Action 1

Once you have opened Outlook Express, look at the e-mail window and familiarise yourself with the buttons and functions illustrated in Figure 3.

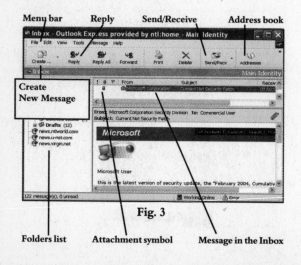

Fig. 3

Menu bar   Reply   Send/Receive   Address book

Create New Message

Folders list   Attachment symbol   Message in the Inbox

The left panel illustrated in Figure. 3 may not resemble the picture on your e-mail window. Don't worry! It simply means that your e-mail has not yet been customised. You can leave the panel as it is or if you would like to change follow the steps in Section 11.

Section 6:
The Folders List

Essential Information

The **Folders List** on the left side of Outlook Express, allows you to file and manage your incoming and outgoing e-mails (Fig. 4). The **Inbox** is used to receive all e-mails. The **Outbox** houses your outgoing mail until you go online to send them. **Sent Items** lists all e-mails successfully sent. When you delete an item it goes into **Deleted Items**. If you wish to compose a message but not send it immediately, it can be placed in the **Drafts** folder to send later (Fig. 5).

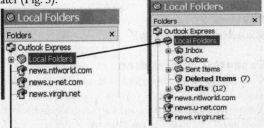

Click on the plus sign by Local Folders to show the Inbox, Outbox, Sent Items, Deleted Items and Drafts

Fig. 4   Fig. 5

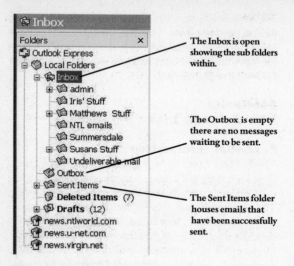

Fig. 6

Section 7: Reading an Email

Essential Information

When messages are received (downloaded) they are placed in the **Inbox** of Outlook Express. Look at Figure 7 and notice that the **Inbox** has been selected and that the right hand panel lists all the e-mails that have been received. At the moment only one e-mail message is listed and that is a welcome message from Microsoft.

Action 1

To read a message, click on **Inbox** in the **Folders list** (left panel). The messages received will be listed in bold text on the right (Fig. 7). Click on the message to highlight and its contents will be displayed in the space below.

Action 2

Double click on the listed message and a larger window opens displaying the message.

Click on Inbox

Click on message
(or double-click to view in larger window.)

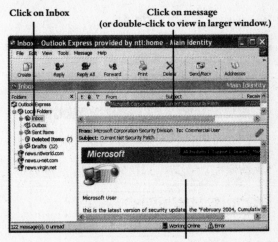

Message is displayed

Fig. 7

Section 8:
Writing a New Message

Action 1

Click on **Create** (Fig. 8) and the new message window opens.

Fig. 8

Action 2

Look at the first part of the message window (Fig. 9).

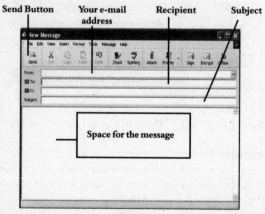

Fig. 9

The window contains various sections or fields, which need to be completed in order to send a message. To type inside a field, move the pointer onto the relevant place and click once. The text cursor will appear and you will be able to type.

From – your email address is entered automatically by Outlook Express.

To – type in the recipients e-mail address.

Cc – (Carbon copy field) type in address if you are sending a copy. If not leave blank.

Subject – give your message a short relevant title.

Click in the large space and type your message.

Click on the **Send** button. If you are working offline the message will be stored in the Outbox until you go online and then it will be sent automatically.

Section 9:
Sending and Receiving an E-mail

Action 1
Click on the **Send/Receive** button on the message window (Fig. 10). You will be invited to connect, if you haven't already done so.

Fig. 10

Action 2

Outlook Express will then check if there are any outgoing or incoming messages. A progress bar will appear showing messages being sent or received (Fig. 11).

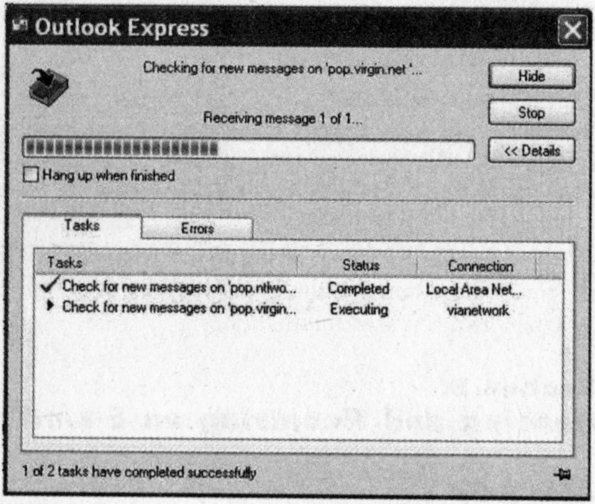

Fig. 11

Action 3
If you are not connected to Broadband, don't forget to disconnect.

Section 10:
Replying to an E-mail

Essential Information
You can reply to a message that has just been received or to a previous message stored in the **Inbox**.

Action 1
Click on the **Reply** button along the top of the e-mail window just below the menu bar (Fig. 7). The sender's e-mail address is automatically inserted into the new e-mail message window and the original message is copied.

When you click on Reply, the From, To, and Subject fields are filled automatically.

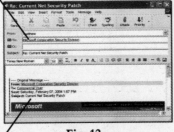

Fig. 12
The sender's message is retained and a space provided at the top for your reply.

Action 2

Type in your own message, retaining any of the key points of the sender's message, that you wish to include. Any text not required can be deleted.

Action 3

Click on the **Send** button. If you are not ready to connect to the Internet, the message can be stored in the Outbox until you next log on.

Section 11:
Customising the Layout of the E-mail Window

Action 1

Open Outlook Express. Click on **View** on the **Menu bar** and a drop-down menu appears. Click on **Layout** as in Figure 13.

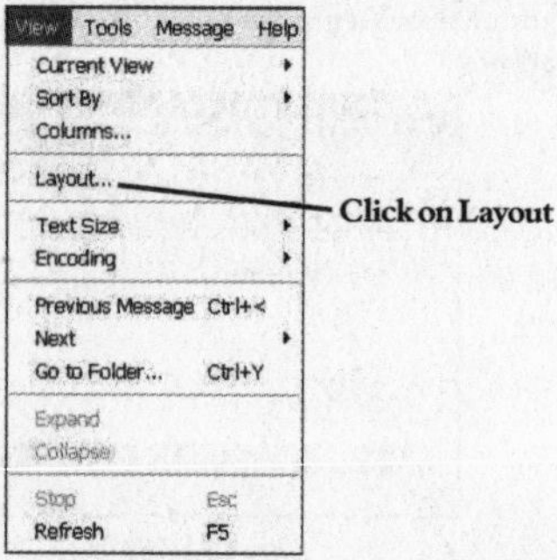

Fig. 13

Action 2

The **Window Layout Properties** dialogue box opens as in Figure 14.

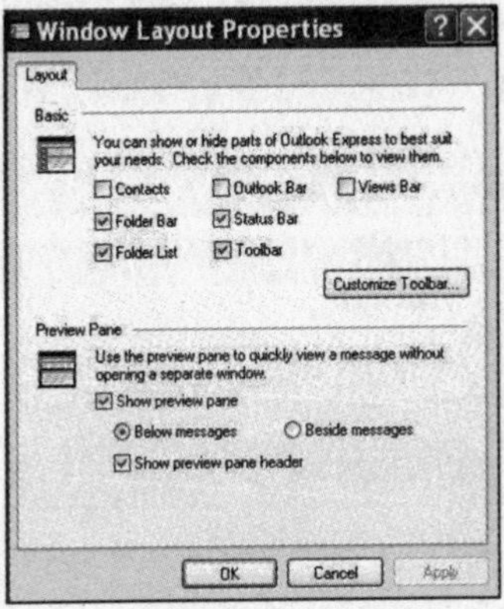

Fig. 14

Action 3

If you want the **Outlook Bar** visible (Fig. 15) make sure that a tick appears in the check box by **Outlook Bar** on the Layout Properties Window (Fig. 5). If it is not, just move the pointer onto the check box and click once. Then make sure that the tick in the check box by the side of Folders list is removed. Then click on **Apply**, then OK.

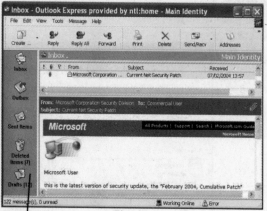

Fig. 15

Outlook Bar

Action 4

If you only want the folders list (Fig. 16) then remove the tick in the check box by **Outlook Bar** and make sure that there is a tick in the check box by **Folders List** (Fig. 14). Then click on **Apply**, then **OK**.

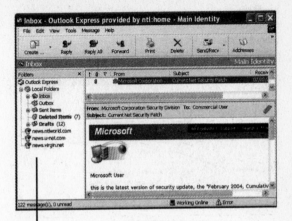

Fig. 16

Folders list

Action 5

If you want both the Outlook Bar and the Folders list visible, make sure that there are ticks in the check boxes by the side of each. Then click on **Apply** and then **OK**.

Section 12: Customising E-mail

Essential Information

It's possible to customise Outlook Express to alter the default settings and change how messages are dealt with, for your convenience.

Action 1

Go to **Tools** on the menu bar, click once and then click on
Options. And the **Options** box opens as in Figure 17.
Select the tab called **General**.

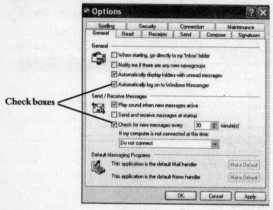

Check boxes

Fig. 17

Action 2

Look at the check boxes on the **Option** box and select
those that you wish to keep. Remember that if you wish to
keep a function then there must be a tick present in the
check box. It is probably a good idea to select **play sound
when new messages arrive**, because this will make you
aware when you have new mail.

Action 3

When you have finished making your selections, don't

336

forget to click on **Apply** and then **OK**.

Section 13:
Deleting

Essential Information

It is not necessary to retain all the messages that you send or receive. It is possible to remove unwanted messages from both the Outbox and the Inbox. In fact it is a good idea to regularly tidy up your mailbox!

Action 1

Select whichever mailbox you are going to tidy.

Action 2

Highlight the e-mail to be removed and then go to **Edit** on the menu bar and click on **Delete** (Fig. 18). To get rid of all your deleted e-mails, go to Edit and select '**Empty 'Deleted items' Folder**, from the drop-down menu.

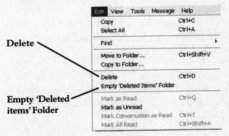

Fig. 18

Section 14:
Attaching Documents or Files

Essential Information

It is possible to attach documents, photographs or files held on your computer to an e-mail. It is often quicker and cheaper than sending them by post. However if your files are large or include graphics or pictures they may take a long time to get through. They will also take the recipient a long time to download.

Action 1

Click on the **Attach** button – it looks like a paper clip.

Fig. 19

Action 2

A box opens called **Insert Attachment** (Fig. 19a). Locate and select your document, click **Attach** and the document is attached to the e-mail (Fig. 20).

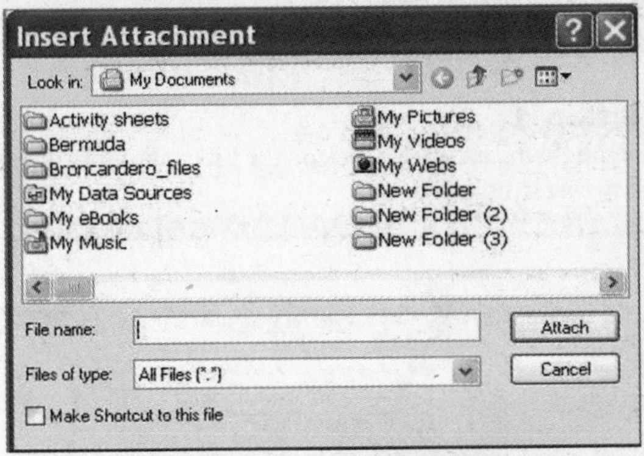

Fig. 19a

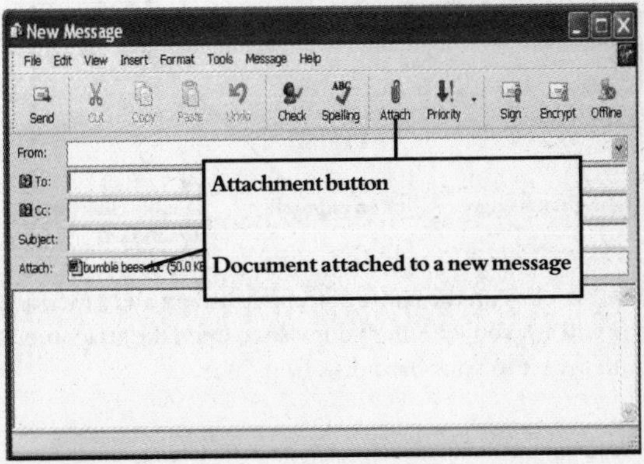

Fig. 20

Section 15:
Opening an Attachment

Action 1

Highlight the message. Click on the paper clip and a drop-down list is displayed.

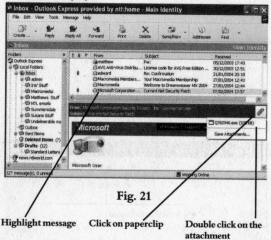

Fig. 21

Highlight message   Click on paperclip   Double click on the attachment

Double click on the name of the attachment and a message box will ask you whether you wish to open the attachment or to save it to your hard disk (Fig. 21a).

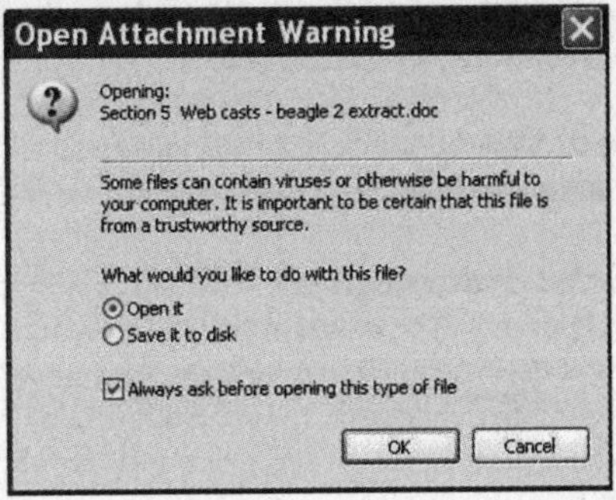

Fig. 21a

Check the **Open it** circle and view the attachment before deciding whether to save it. **Be very wary of opening attachments from people you do not know. An e-mail attachment is one of the most common methods of spreading computer virus.**

Section 16:
Sending Messages to Several People

Essential Information

Look back to Figure 12 and notice in the top part of the window a field called Cc (carbon copy). To send a message to several people, type one address in the **To** field and the rest in the **Cc** field. Separate them by a semicolon and a space. When your e-mail is sent, each person will receive a copy of the message and they will all be able to see who else received a copy.

Section 17:
Address book

Essential Information

Outlook Express can be programmed to automatically add addresses to the Address Book. Look back at Figure 16 you see a button called **Addresses**. By clicking on this you can add e-mail addresses, works address, phone numbers and much more.

Action 1

Click on **Tools** on the menu bar and from the drop-down menu select **Options** (Fig. 22). Click to add a tick to the check box by the words, **Automatically put people I reply to in my Address Book**. When you receive an email the senders address automatically enters the address book.

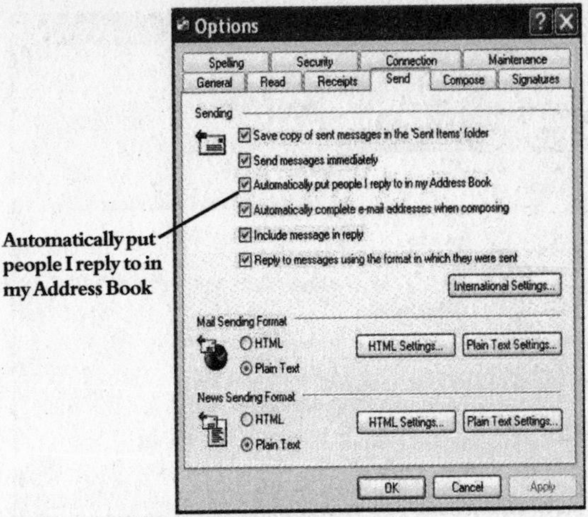

Automatically put people I reply to in my Address Book

Fig. 22

Section 18:
Adding an Address Manually

Action 1

Double click on a message that you have received. Highlight the e-mail address (this is next to **From**) and right click on the mouse button. Click on **Add to Address Book** on the drop-down list.

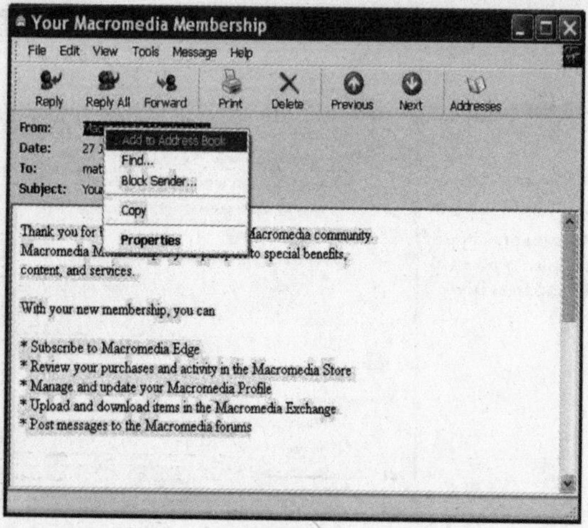

Fig. 23

Action 2

The **Properties** dialogue box opens and the **Summary** tab displays the name and e-mail address of the contact (Fig. 24). If you wish to add more details about this contact, click on the **Name** tab and enter the information in the text boxes shown.

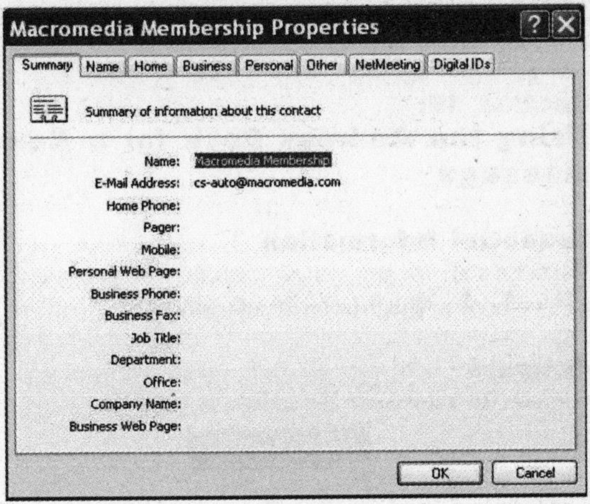

Fig. 24

Action 3

To add the address of person who has not already sent you
an e-mail, go to **File** and click on **New Contact**.

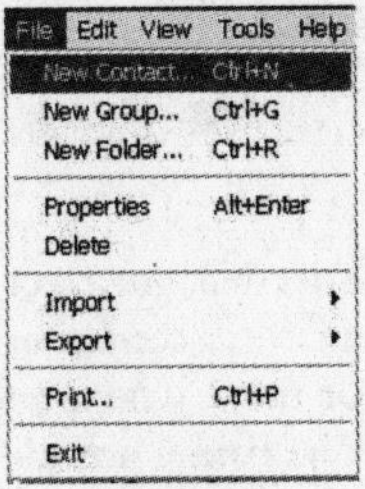

Fig. 25

The **Name** tab of the Properties dialogue box is displayed and you can enter the relevant details in the text boxes.

Section 19:
Using the Address Book for a New Message

Essential Information
When you are writing a new message, you can use the address book to enter the recipient's addresses.

Action 1
Click on the symbol for the address book by **To**.

Click on the Address book symbol —

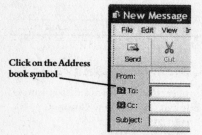

Fig. 26

Action 2
The **Select Recipients** dialogue box opens (Fig. 27). For the main recipient click on a contact in the Name list, and then click on **To** For those who are to receive a carbon copy, click on **Cc**. The names are added to the Message recipients lists. When you have finished click on **OK**.

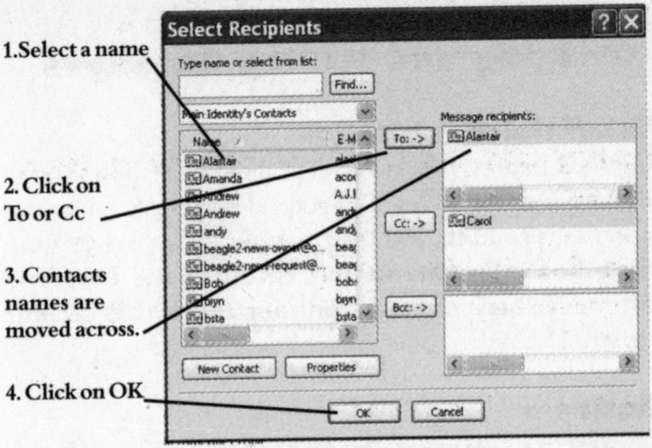

1. Select a name

2. Click on To or Cc

3. Contacts names are moved across.

4. Click on OK

Fig. 27

Action 3

The contacts have been entered into your new e-mail message).

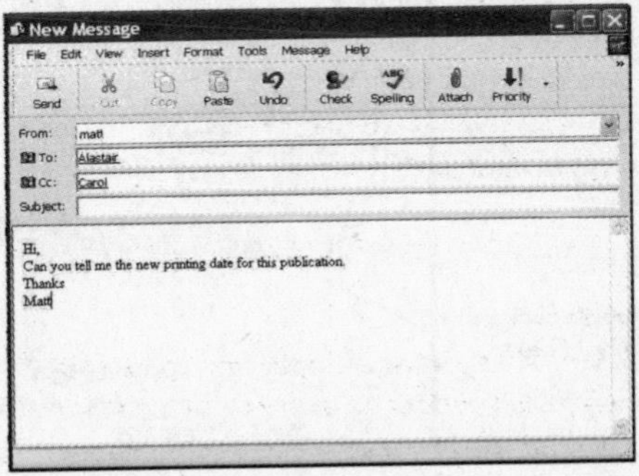

Fig. 28

Section 20:
Managing and Moving Messages

Essential Information

Outlook Express is a powerful program that allows you to manage your messages. It's a good idea to create folders for important contacts and then transfer the messages from the **Inbox** or **Sent items** into relevant folders. Do get rid of unnecessary messages or your Inbox will become very full.

Action 1

To create a folder, select the destination (click on Inbox or Sent items etc.), *right* click on the mouse button and a drop-down list appears.

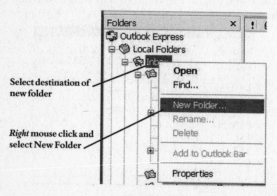

Fig. 29

Click on **New Folder** and the **Create Folder** box is displayed.

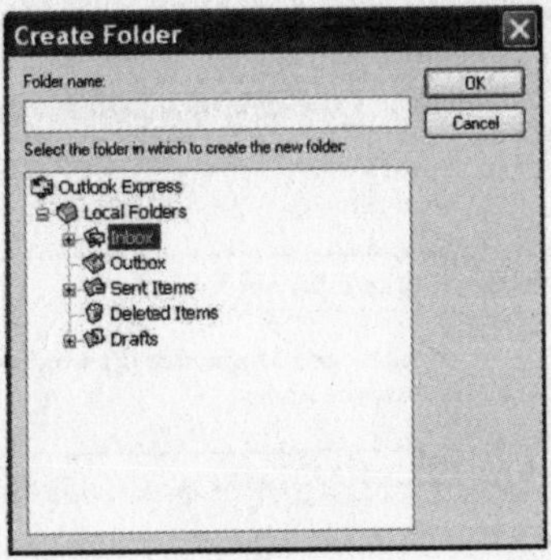

Fig. 30

Type in a name for the folder and then click **OK**.

Action 2

To move messages into the folder, highlight the message on the right of the Outlook Express window and then click and drag it into the folder in the folders list. When the folder turns blue, release the button and the message will have been placed (or dropped) into its new position.

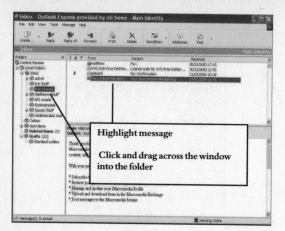

Highlight message

Click and drag across the window into the folder

Fig. 31

Section 21:
Blocking Unwanted Emails

Essential Information

If you receive any unwanted emails, future messages from the same sender can be placed directly into the recycle bin by using the blocked senders list.

Action 1

Click on the unwanted email and then click on **Message** in the Outlook Express window. From the drop down menu select **Block Sender**.

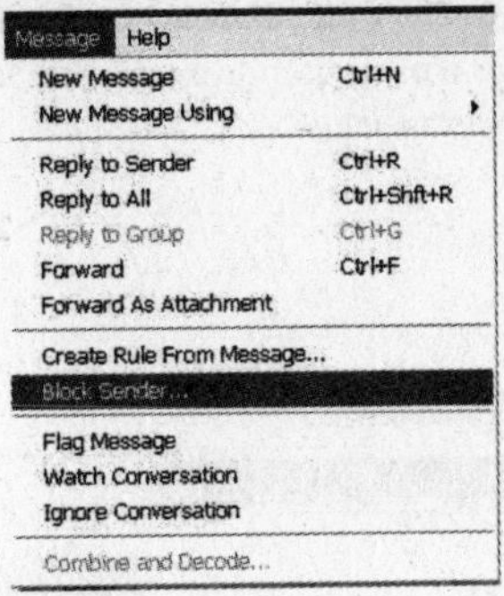

Message	Help	
New Message		Ctrl+N
New Message Using		▶
Reply to Sender		Ctrl+R
Reply to All		Ctrl+Shift+R
Reply to Group		Ctrl+G
Forward		Ctrl+F
Forward As Attachment		
Create Rule From Message...		
Block Sender...		
Flag Message		
Watch Conversation		
Ignore Conversation		
Combine and Decode...		

Fig. 32

Action 2

A message box will confirm the e-mail address which has been added to the blocked senders list and asks 'Would you like to remove all messages from this sender from the current folder now?' (Fig. 33). Now click on **Yes**.

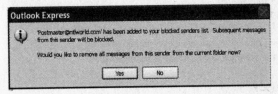

Outlook Express

ⓘ 'Postmaster@ntlworld.com' has been added to your blocked senders list. Subsequent messages from this sender will be blocked.

Would you like to remove all messages from this sender from the current folder now?

[Yes]   [No]

Fig. 33

Action 3

To view the Blocked Senders List go to **Tools** on the

Outlook Express window and on the drop-down menu select **Message Rules**, then from the sub menu click on **Blocked Senders List**.

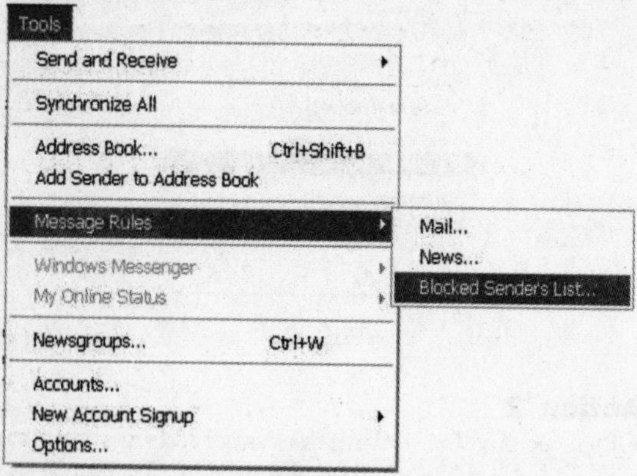

Fig. 34

Action 4

The Message Rules dialogue box displays all those on the list. Click on an address to **Modify** or **Remove**. To add an address manually click on the **Add** button and type in the e-mail address in the text box provided.

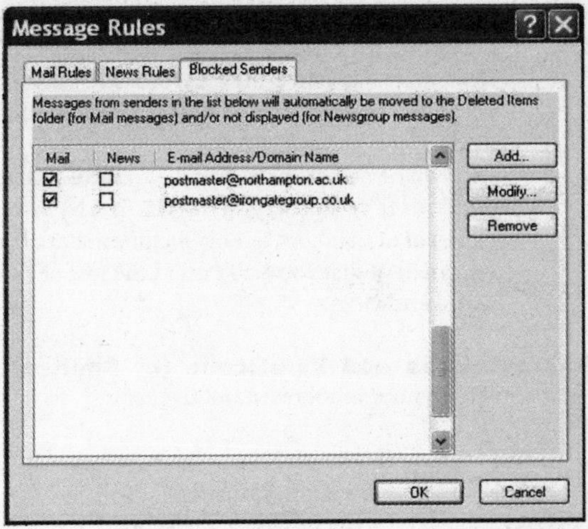

Fig. 35

Section 22:
E-mail Etiquette

Essential Information

1. Keep your message short and to the point. Remember someone else has got to pay to download your piece of prose!

2. E-mails are not conventional letters so you do not need to write them like one – don't give your home address or the date.

3. DON'T SHOUT! That is, do not type your message in capital letters. It is considered rude.

353

4.   Give your message a subject; it helps the recipient to manage their files.

5.   Remember that your e-mails can be read by anyone who has access to your computer so be polite and discrete.

6.   Once an e-mail has been sent it enters the public domain. It could then be forwarded by your recipient onto others, so only include material or information that you don't mind the rest of the world knowing.

Abbreviations and Emoticons (or Smilies)

Here are some common abbreviations in emails:

BTW	By the way
FYI	For your information
FAQ	Frequently asked questions
IMHO	In my humble opinion
TIA	Thanks in advance
IOW	In other words

Smilies are little pictures that help to convey meaning to your e-mail. They are also called emoticons. Use the normal letters and symbols on the keyboard, i.e. colon, semicolon, brackets etc, to create the following examples of smilies.

:-) Happy   :-(Sad   :-II Angry
;-) Wink   :-D Laughing :-I Not amused

If you can't see the connection between the smiley and its meaning, turn the page sideways.

Chapter Eleven:
How to Keep Your Computer Healthy

Section 1:
Staying Dust Free

Essential Information

Your systems unit is designed to be insulated against outside interference. However it is still possible to 'inject' dust into the system via the floppy disk and the CD or DVD.

Consequently the disks should be kept as clean as possible. Not only to maintain a 'healthy' computer but also to protect the information that is stored on your disks. Dust or grit within the floppy can damaged it irreparably and likewise finger marks or dirt on a CD/DVD.

Here are a few DO's and DON'Ts:

DO hold a CD or DVD by the edges and keep it in the wallet or case provided.

DON'T put your floppy disks, CDs or DVDs loose in your pocket or bag – at the very least pop it into an envelope to keep it clean.

DO remember to dust your monitor screen. It is not good for your eyesight to be peering at the screen through a fog.

DON'T drop coffee or any other drink over the keyboard – it makes the keys stick.

DO keep your systems unit free from a build-up of dust. Special wipes to clean the systems unit are available from your local computer store or use a similar dust free cloth.

Section 2: Tidiness

Essential Information

Computer tidiness begins once you start creating documents and saving them onto your floppy disks and the hard drive. If you fail to organise you may find you waste precious time trying to locate an item. It is also very frustrating!

Action 1

Give all documents or files that you save an appropriate and logical name. Including a date is also useful. Collect together similar files into a folder. As you add documents to a floppy disk or CD, write the file name on the disk label as soon as the disk is ejected.

Action 2

You need to be able to manage your documents and files. Read *Chapter Seven: Create and Manage Files* and then set aside some time to get yourself organised!

Section 3:
How to Escape or Close Down

Jamming / Frozen Screen

When you are busy working on the computer you may sometimes, without realising, open up too many windows or programs on the screen. Sometimes this may cause the computer to jam. On other occasions an item of software may not be particularly robust and cause the PC to crash.

What could be the consequences?

1. The screen may 'freeze'.
2. The mouse may stop working.
3. It may not be possible to close down any windows.
4. You are left with a screen full of material and no way of extricating from the jam.

Top Tip

Always save your work **as you go along**. You never know when the computer may crash, a power cut or power surge may occur or even when someone may accidentally pull out the PC plug.

Action 1

You will need to escape from this situation and close down. The keyboard is able to provide you with an alternative way of moving around the screen. Look at your keyboard diagram and identify these keys.

Control (Ctrl)
Escape (Esc)
Cursor keys
Tab key
Return/Enter
The Microsoft Windows logo key

Action 2

Press the Microsoft Windows logo key and the menu from the **Start** button should appear.

Or

Press **Control** and, whilst holding the key down, press **Escape.** The menu from the **Start** button should appear.

In both cases use the cursor key to highlight **Turn Off Computer** on the Start menu and then press Enter. The **Turn Off Computer** box will appear.

Use the cursor keys to select **Turn Off.** Press Enter. The computer may (if you're lucky) ask you if you want to save your work. If so, use the **Tab key** to select Yes. The computer, once it has saved any files, will proceed to close down.

Top Tip
It's probably a good idea to practise this emergency escape/close down procedure **before** you actually need it.

Section 4:
What is a Computer Virus?

Jargon Buster
Computer Virus

A virus is a damaging piece of code. Once the virus infects a computer it can corrupt the programs on the system and either be just an irritant or very corrupting.

There are three ways of acquiring an unwelcome computer virus.

1. They come attached to e-mails.
2. They can come attached to a floppy disk that has been used on another computer.
3. They can also be downloaded, without you realising, when logging on to the Internet.

Section 5:
Preventing Virus Infection

Essential Information

By exercising a few simple precautions it is possible to reduce the risk of a computer virus infection.

Action 1

If you receive an e-mail from anyone you do not know and it has an attachment, the best thing to do with it is place it,

unopened, in the Recycle Bin, or delete it completely from
your system.

Action 2

Do not interchange floppy disks between home and the
workplace as this is a common way of introducing and
spreading virus.

Action 3

Keep backup disks of your files. If anything happens to
your PC hard drive, then you will not have lost all your
work.

Jargon Buster
Backup disks
A floppy disk or CD copy of your files which you
keep on your computer hard drive.

Action 4

Install an anti-virus program – see Section 6 and be aware
of the files and programs that should be scanned by your
anti virus program. These are:

1. Any files or programs that have attachments.
2. Any files or programs that have little 'macro
   programs' (a small program that works within a
   program)
3. Any floppy or rewritable CDs from a third party
   should be checked by your anti-virus software
   prior to loading any information onto your

machine. Your anti-virus program will carry instructions on how to do this.

Your virus checking program will tell you whenever it detects a virus and can usually 'kill' or isolate any it finds.

Section 6:
Anti-Virus Software

Essential Information

All owners of computers should invest in an anti-virus program. It will sit there behind the scenes waiting to scan a file or program for a virus. You can buy a program (Action 1) or download a free version from the Internet (Action 2).

Action 1

There are a number of ant-virus programs which you can purchase, readily available from your local computer store. When you have made your selection place the disk in the computer and follow the instructions as they appear on your screen.

Action 2

You can also download anti-virus software from the Internet. Many allow you a free trial before you buy, for example free downloads are offered to home users only, at the following site:

http://www.grisoft.com/us/us_dwnl_free.php

There are many more anti-virus programs on the Internet so if you want to check them out open up your search engine and type in 'anti-virus'. The following are two well-known brands. More information from:

Norton Antivirus from:
http://www.symantic.com/avcenter/index.html

McAfee Virus Scan from:
http://www.mcafee.com

These can all be regularly updated from the programs web site, so that your virus program will always be able to deal with the latest threat.

Action 3

Once you have installed your anti-virus program it will generally automatically scan your computer at regular intervals, inform you of the virus status of your computer and advise you when it is time to update the program to deal with the latest virus threats.

Top Tip

Keep up to date. Get the very latest issue of an anti-virus program, as it will be able to deal with the most recent releases of virus. If you do get a virus that a conventional anti-virus program cannot deal with, you can return your new computer to your dealer and they will wipe the hard disk clean. However, you will loose all the work you have saved onto the hard disk. Keep a backup of all important information.

Section 7:
System Restore

Essential Information

Sometimes, despite all your efforts, you may find occasions when your computer doesn't work properly. Programs, for example may not respond or your system may be operating very slowly. Check first that you do not have a virus by using your anti-virus program. If the problem remains, then **System Restore** allows you to re-set your system to a previous date when it was working normally. You do not lose any of your recent work when you use System Restore.

Action 1

Click on the **Start** button and go to **All Programs**. Select **Accessories**, then **System Tools,** and finally click on **System Restore.**

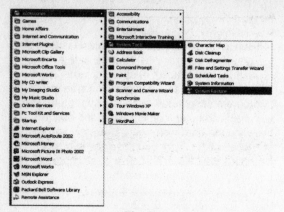

Fig. 1

Action 2

The **System Restore** welcome window opens (Fig. 2). On the right-hand side of the window are three radio buttons. Select the one next to **Restore my computer to an earlier time**. Click **Next**.

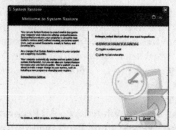

Fig. 2

Action 3

Select a Restore Point opens (Fig. 3). Look at the calendar on the left side of the window. Some of the dates are in bold. These are the dates for which Windows XP has created a restore point. Decide when your computer last worked correctly and then click on a bold date which corresponds. On the right of the window select a restore point. There may only be one restore point listed. Click **Next**.

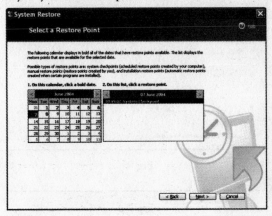

Fig. 3

Action 4

The next window (Fig. 4) asks you to confirm the restore point that you have chosen. It will also list any changes that will be undone. For example if you have installed a new piece of software. Consider if you wish to continue, and if you do, click **Next**. If you do not, click on the **Cancel** button. If you click on Next, Windows XP will start to restore your system.

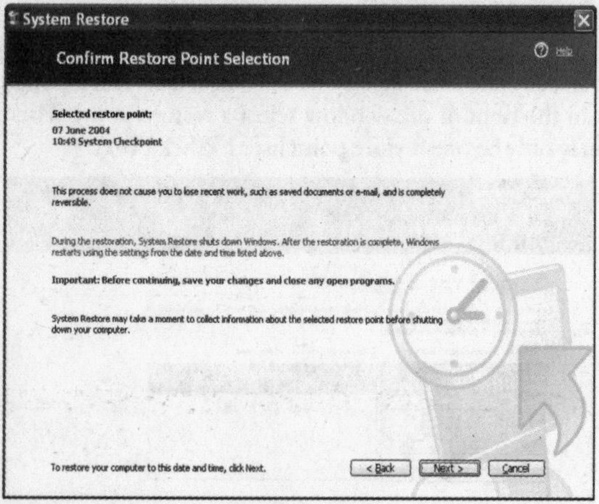

Fig. 4

Top Tip

It's worthwhile learning more about System Restore. Open up System Restore as described in Action 1 and click on Help in the top right corner of the Welcome window.

Section 8:
Disk Space

Essential Information

As you add programs, files and documents to your computer, it's a good idea to review periodically how much free space remains on your hard disk. Checking is a very simple procedure.

Action 1

Click on the **My Computer** icon on your desktop or go to the Start menu and click on **My Computer.** *Right* click on the **Hard Disk Drive** (Fig. 5) and a drop-down menu appears. Click on **Properties**.

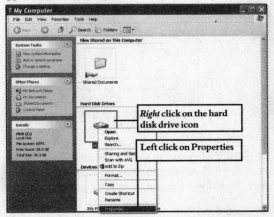

Fig. 5

Action 2

The **HDD** (Hard Disk Drive) **Properties** dialogue box opens (Fig. 6). Click on the **General** tab, if not already opened (Fig. 6). Here you can clearly see how much free and used space there is on the hard drive.

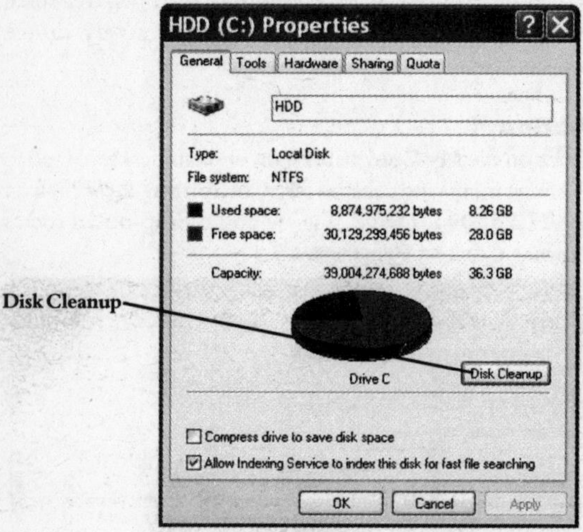

Fig. 6

It may be a good idea to clean up your disk by deleting unwanted files and thus increase the amount of available space. To do this follow the steps in the next section.

Section 9:
Disk Cleanup

Essential Information

When you use **Disk Cleanup**, you will be deleting files. Make sure that you really do wish to remove these files as, once they are gone, they cannot be retrieved.

Action 1

Follow actions 1–2 in Section 8 above and then click on the button called **Disk Cleanup** (Fig. 6).

The following progress bar (Fig. 7) will appear while Disk Cleanup calculates how the amount of space which can be created by cleaning up the hard disk.

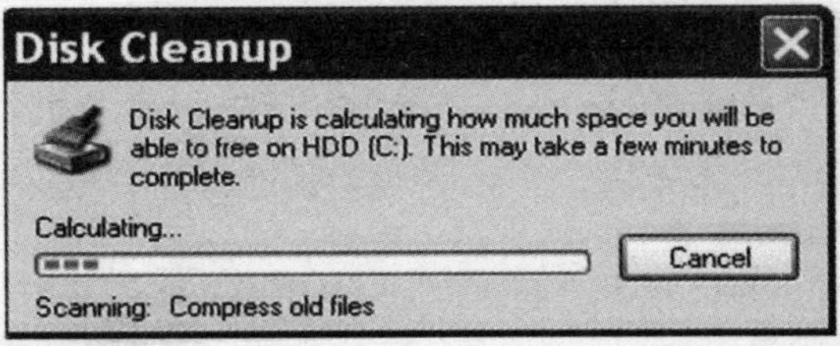

Disk Cleanup   ⊠

Disk Cleanup is calculating how much space you will be able to free on HDD (C:). This may take a few minutes to complete.

Calculating...

▮▮▮▮ | Cancel |

Scanning: Compress old files

Fig. 7

Action 2

The Disk Cleanup dialogue box (Fig. 8) displays the amount of space you can gain. If you are unsure about deletion, select a group and click on View Files.

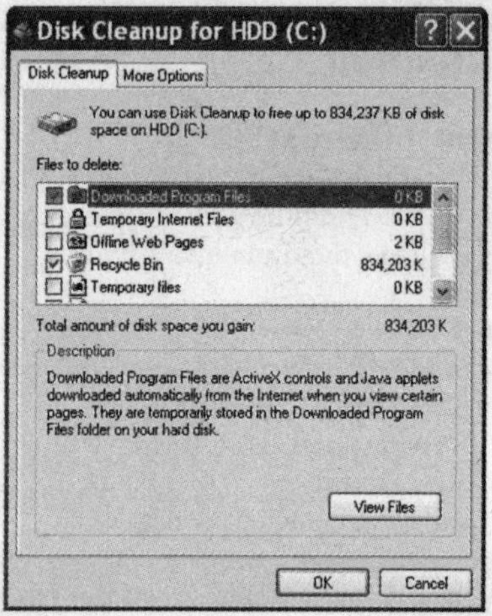

Fig. 8

Action 3

To delete files, click on the check boxes by the groups of files to be deleted and then click **OK.** You will be asked to confirm deletion (Fig. 9). Click on **Yes** and the files will be removed. Click on **No** and the action will be cancelled.

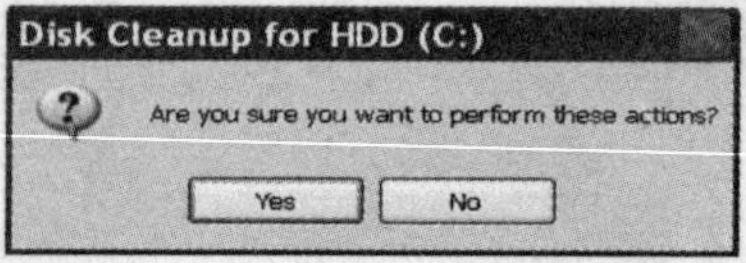

Fig. 9

Section 10:
ScanDisk: Finding and Fixing Errors

Essential Information

ScanDisk is a program which you can use to check your hard disk for errors or damage. It's a good idea to do this periodically as, despite all your good efforts, the hard disk does sometimes get damaged. Besides scanning your disk for problems ScanDisk can also automatically fix them.

Action 1

Click on the **My Computer** icon on your desktop or go to the Start menu and click on **My Computer**. *Right* click on the **Hard Disk Drive,** and a drop-down menu appears. Click on **Properties** (Fig. 5).

Action 2

Click on the **Tools** tab of the Properties dialogue box.

Action 3

Click on the Check Now button

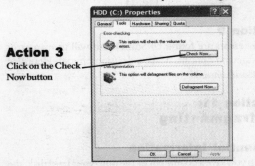

Fig. 10

Action 4

The **Check Disk** dialogue box opens (Fig. 11). Click on the check boxes to select both options: **Automatically fix file system errors** and **Scan for and attempt recovery of bad sectors**. Click on **Start** and ScanDisk will begin to scan and repair your hard disk.

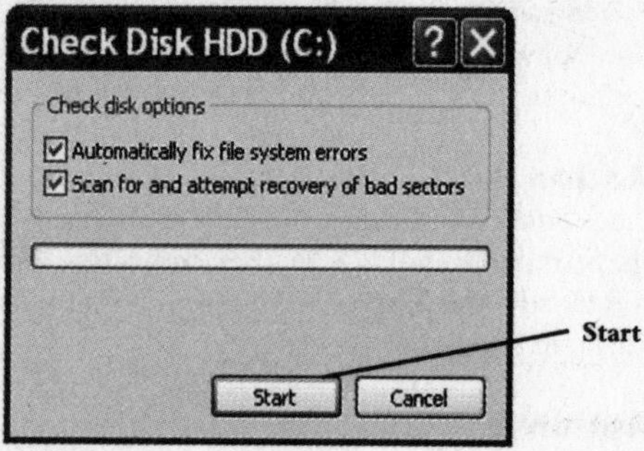

Check Disk HDD (C:)   ？ ✕

Check disk options

☑ Automatically fix file system errors
☑ Scan for and attempt recovery of bad sectors

─────────────── Start

[Start]   [Cancel]

Fig. 11

Action 5

If any errors are found by ScanDisk it will give an error message and options. Make a decision on each identified error as it is listed.

Section 11: Defragmenting

Essential Information

When you save a document or file onto your hard disk, the computer does not necessarily save it all in the same place.

A file could in theory be located in many fragments, in dozens of places on your hard disk. This is because the computer will use the first available space to place a file and then save the rest elsewhere. After a period of time this fragmenting of files will slow up the operation of the computer. **Defragmenting** collects and groups all the separate pieces of individual files, together into one place on the hard disk. This is a very simple procedure.

Top Tip

It's a good idea to defragment your hard disk on a regular basis as part of the general maintenance of your computer system.

Action 1

Click on the **My Computer** icon on your desktop or go to the Start menu and click on **My Computer.** *Right* click on the **Hard Disk Drives** icon and a drop-down menu appears. Click on **Properties** (Fig. 5).

Action 2

Click on the **Tools** tab of the **Properties** dialogue box (Fig. 12). Click on the **Defragment Now** button.

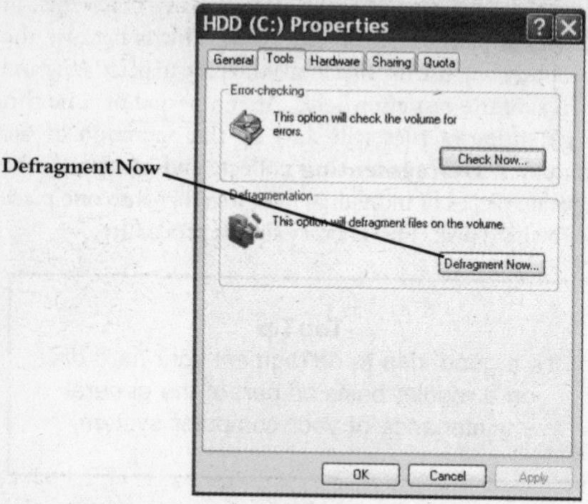

Fig. 12

The **Disk Defragmenter** window opens.

Jargon Buster
Defrag
An abbreviation for defragmenting – used by old computer hands.

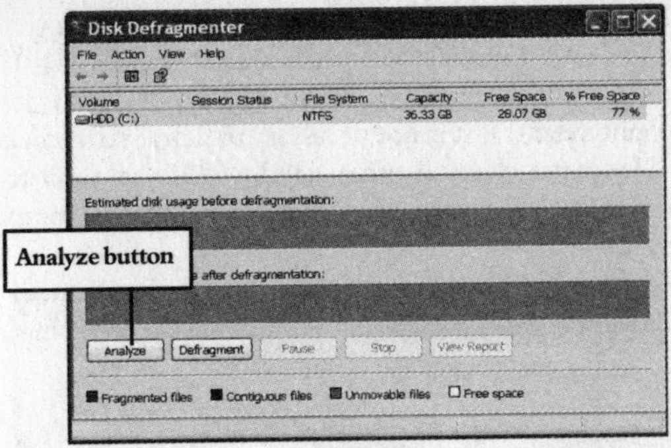

Fig. 13

Action 3

To establish whether it is necessary for you to defragment your disk, click on the **Analyze** button (Fig. 13). The program will analyse the usage of the hard disk and the progress bar will show the level of file defragmentation (Fig. 14).

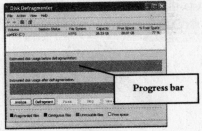

Fig. 14

Once analysis is complete a dialogue box will inform you whether or not to defragment the hard disk (Fig. 15) If you wish, you can click on **View Report** and read the resultant details. If it is not necessary to defragment click on **Close** and close all other windows. If you wish to continue to defragment, then click on the **Defragment** button.

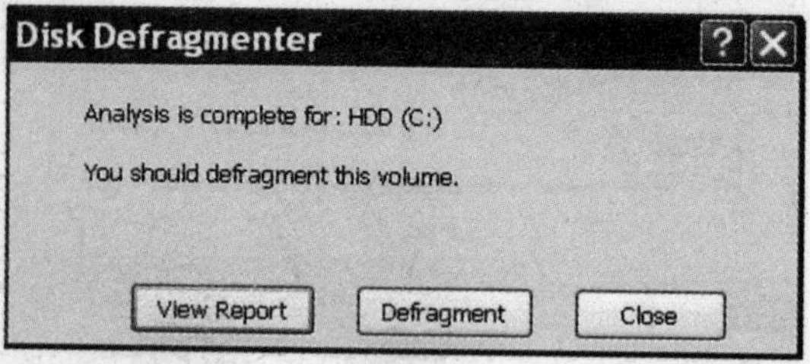

Disk Defragmenter ? X

Analysis is complete for: HDD (C:)

You should defragment this volume.

View Report   Defragment   Close

Fig. 15

Action 4

It will take a few minutes to complete the process. As the Disk Defragmenter program operates, the lower progress bar shows the files being grouped together (Fig. 16).

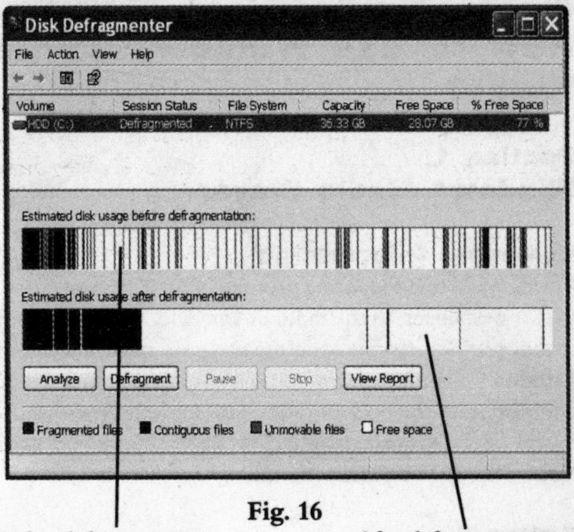

Fig. 16

Before defragmentation   After defragmentation

Action 5

The program will inform you when the process has finished. If you wish you can view a report by clicking on **View Report**. Otherwise, close this window.

Chapter Twelve:
How to Use Windows Media Player

Section 1:
Windows Media Player

Essential Information
Windows Media Player is a program which enables you to play music, listen to the radio or view video clips on your computer. Before you open the program make sure your computer is equipped with speakers or headphones. These will plug into the back of the computer. Windows Media Player can be opened straight from the desktop shortcut or from the **All Programs** menu.

Action 1
Find the icon (Fig. 1).on the desktop for **Windows Media Player**, and double-click. Windows Media Player will open.

Windows
Media
Player

Fig. 1

Or

Click once on **Start,** and then go to **All Programs,** then **Windows Media Player** and click once. **Windows Media**

Player will then open (Fig. 2).

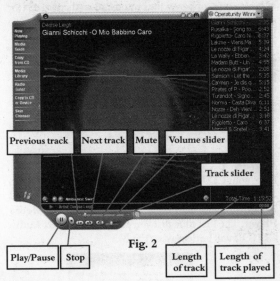

Previous track | Next track | Mute | Volume slider

Track slider

Fig. 2

Play/Pause | Stop

Length of track | Length of track played

Section 2:
Control Buttons

Essential Information

There are five buttons and two slider controls at the bottom of Windows Media Player. These allow you to start, stop, pause, access the previous or next track, turn the sound on or off, adjust volume, and move the track forward or backwards.

Action 1

Move your pointer over the buttons, allow them to rest for a moment and a label will appear, identifying each button (Fig. 2).

Section 3:
Playing a Music CD

Essential Information

You do not need to open Windows Media Player first in order to play a CD. It should Autorun.

Action 1

Place your CD into the correct tray or drive. It should run automatically but if it does not, then go to **Start, All Programs** and then click once on **Windows Media Player.** The first time that you play a CD, the box **Audio CD (Q:)** will be displayed (Fig. 3).

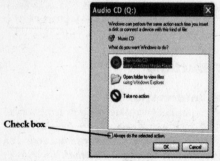

Check box

Fig. 3

Make sure **Play Audio CD using Windows Media Player** is highlighted and then click OK. Windows Media Player will appear on the screen and the music will begin.

Top Tip

If you wish you can stop the Audio CD (Q:) box from appearing. Make sure that **Play Audio CD using Windows Media Player** is highlighted and click on the check box; Then click OK (Fig. 3). This will mean that Windows Media Player will always automatically appear when you open it from the desktop or Start menu.

Section 4;
Tuning into a Radio Station

Essential Information
Windows Media Player allows you to tune into a huge array of world wide radio stations. In order to do this, however, you must be connected to the Internet and that means using the telephone and incurring telephone charges.

Action 1
Connect to the Internet and open Windows Media Payer from your desktop or Start menu.

Action 2

On the left-hand pane of Windows Media Player, click on
Radio Tuner. The centre of the player will go black and
the word **'Loading'** will appear. Wait a few moments until
this loading process is completed. Your Media Player will
then list the options available to you as in Fig. 4.

Top Tip
Don't forget that besides the volume control
on the Windows Media Player you can also
adjust the volume of your speakers.

Search for a
specific subject

Radio Tuner
button

Search for more
stations that cover
types of music.

List of world wide
Radio Station's
available

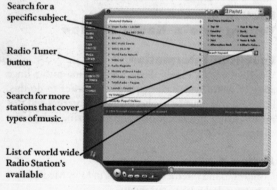

Fig. 4

Action 3

Select an option or a radio station that appeals to you, and double-click. We chose **Classic Rock** from the **Find more Stations** list of options. Whatever you choose, further details about the station are displayed (Fig. 5). Click on **Play**. This opens a new window for that particular station (Fig. 6) and the music will begin!

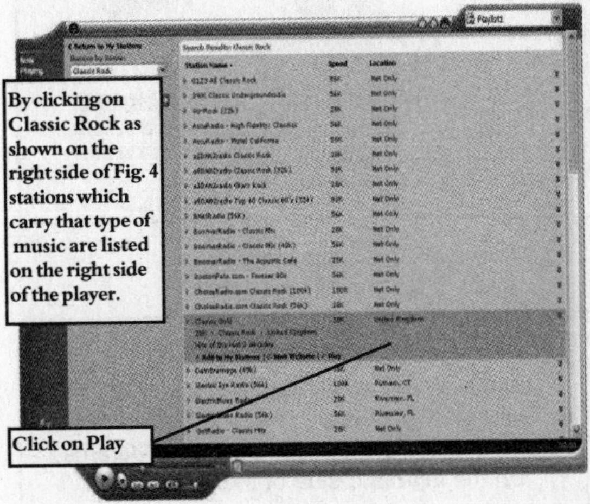

By clicking on Classic Rock as shown on the right side of Fig. 4 stations which carry that type of music are listed on the right side of the player.

Click on Play

Fig. 5

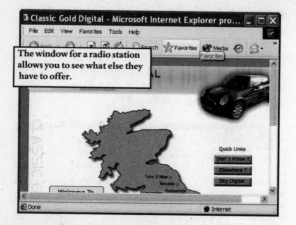

The window for a radio station allows you to see what else they have to offer.

Fig. 6

Top Tip
If you use Windows Media Player a lot, you will find that the program will be automatically listed among the frequently used programs, on the left-hand side of the Start menu.

Section 5:
Viewing a Webcast

Essential Information
Windows Media Player can be used to watch live or archived

web casts. The one shown in Figure 8 is of a press conference for the Beagle 2 team (mission to Mars). To view a webcast you need to connect to the Internet, so once again remember, you will be incurring telephone charges. The following actions will show you how we viewed a Beagle 2 webcast.

Action 1

We connected to the Internet and typed in the web address http://beagle2.com, in the address bar of Internet Explorer. When the home page had downloaded we double-clicked on **Watch live webcast from the media briefings**. Another window opened called '**beagle 2: video album**'.

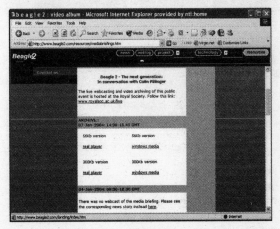

Fig. 7

Action 2

We scrolled down and selected an archive. The one shown in Figure 7 is for 07–Jan–2004. We double clicked on Windows Media, just below 56Kb version, and the archive opened on Windows Media Player (Fig. 8).

Fig. 8

Action 3

We waited for a few moments while the connection was made and the 'buffering' completed. The webcast then started to run automatically. The control buttons at the bottom of the player allowed adjustment of the clip.

Action 4

Like many web pages, webcasts are not permanent 'fixtures' and may close or alter through time. If the Beagle 2 webcast is not available try to access another by going to the European Space Agency, Mars Express web site at:

http://www.esa.int/SPECIALS/Mars_Express/index.htm.

Under Multimedia, select from Mars Express videos or HRSC videos and choose to view with Windows Media

Section 6:
Choosing a Skin

Essential Information

The Windows Media Player takes up a lot of room on the desktop, but it is possible to reduce its size.

Action 1

Click on **Skin Chooser** and a list of options appears (Fig. 9). Click on any one and a preview appears on the right side of the Windows Media Player. The one we have chosen is called **Classic XP**.

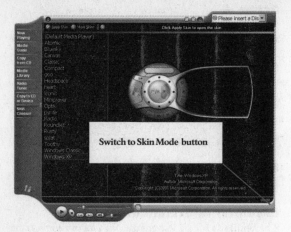

Switch to Skin Mode button

Fig. 9

Action 2

Click on the button called **Switch to Skin Mode** (Fig. 9). The large screen disappears and the smaller version (Fig. 10) which you have chosen now sits on the desktop. Look at Figure 10 for the control buttons on a skin.

Action 3

Move your pointer over the buttons, allow them to rest for a moment and a label will appear, identifying each button.

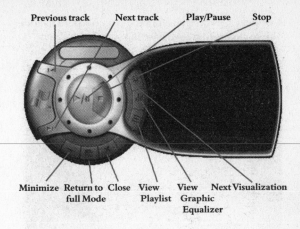

Fig. 10

Section 7: Visualizations

Essential Information:

These are patterns which are displayed on Windows Player while your music is playing. It is possible to select various styles from the visualization menu. The visualization buttons are identified on Figure 11.

Action 1

While you are listening to your music, click on the visualization menu and select a new style, which will then appear on the Player. Click on the next visualization button

to view the next design within the chosen style. There are
loads to choose from – so have fun!

Show Menu Bar button

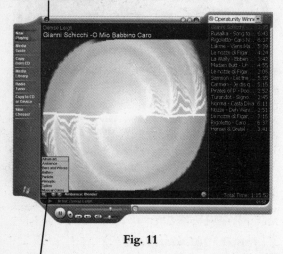

Fig. 11

**Visualization button – click here for a list of styles. Click on Next
Visualization for more designs within a style.**

The current visualization is called Ambience: Blender

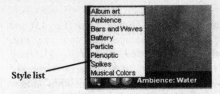

Style list

Fig. 11a

Section 8:
More about Windows Media Player

Essential Information
To find our more it is a good idea to go on a Windows Media Tour. To do this you need to access **Help**.

Action 1
Look at Figure 11 and identify the location of the **Show Menu Bar** button. Click once and the menu bar is displayed. Go to **Help** on the menu bar and click on **Help Topics** (Fig. 12).

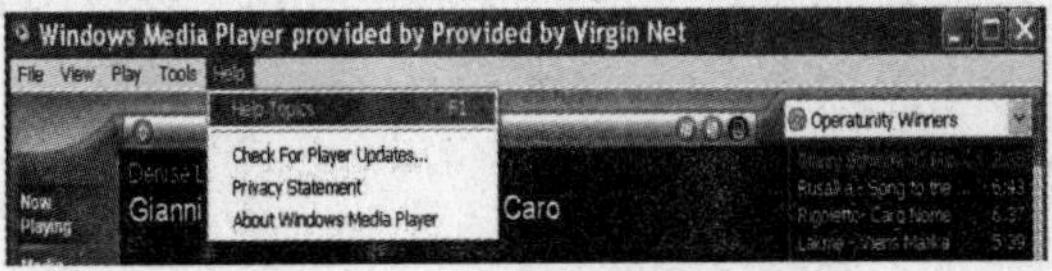

Fig. 12

Action 2

Click on **Windows Media Player Tour** (Fig. 13) and
then follow the on-screen instructions. Or you may wish
to click on **Using Windows Media Player** (Fig. 13) which
provides instructions on how to use the main features of
the Player. Both will give you useful information on how
to get the best out of your Player.

Windows Media Player Tour

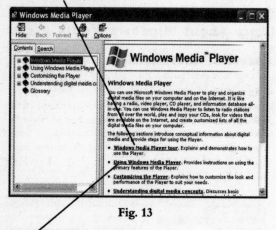

Fig. 13

Using Windows Media Player

This Help function can give you more information about
the following useful features.

How to Use Windows Media Player

The Media Guide
This allows you to explore the latest music, movie trailers and news. Click on the Media Guide button and connect to the Internet. Follow the on-screen instructions.

Copy from CD
This allows you to copy a track from a CD onto your computer's hard disk. This then allows a track to be played at a later date, without inserting the original CD. You should be aware, however, of the copyright implications.

Media Library
This is a good way of organising your favourite music and video clips.

Video Clips
Windows Media Player can be used to view movie trailer clips or home movies. These can be imported from the Internet or from your digital camera.

Chapter Thirteen:
How to Add a Scanner and a Digital Camera

Section 1:
Setting up a Scanner

Essential Information

Windows XP can usually find and set up a scanner automatically. Just plug in the scanner's cable into the computer terminal and Windows will automatically install it for you. If this does not work, you will need to use the **Scanner and Camera Installation Wizard** (see Section 4 below).

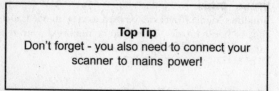

Top Tip
Don't forget - you also need to connect your scanner to mains power!

Section 2:
Setting up a Digital Camera

Essential Information

Windows XP can also find and set up a digital camera. Plug the camera's cable into the computer terminal and Windows will automatically install it for you. If this does not work, you will need to use the Scanner and Camera Installation Wizard (see Section 4 below). Once your camera has been set up you can use the camera software or the software installed on your computer to download the photographs from the camera onto the computer.

Section 3:
Scanner and Camera Software

Essential Information

There are a number of programs which enable you to download and edit your digital photographs or pictures from your scanner. Two of the most popular are Photo Express and Picture It but there are others available. You may find them as part of your computer package or they may come with the scanner or camera that you purchase. Follow the instructions which come with your particular software.

Section 4:
The Scanner and Camera
Installation Wizard

Essential Information

If your computer has failed to find either your newly installed scanner or digital camera, then you will need to use the Scanner and Camera Installation Wizard. The same procedure is used for both pieces of hardware. You will need to know the manufacturer and make of each device in order to make the correct selection when prompted by the wizard.

Action 1

Go to the **Start** menu and click on **Control Panel**.

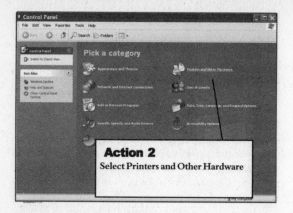

Fig. 1

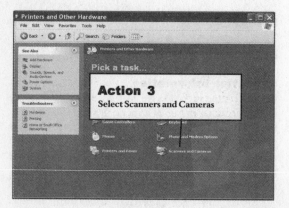

Fig. 2

How to Add a Scanner and a Digital Camera

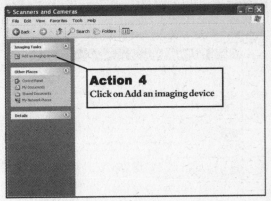

Fig. 3

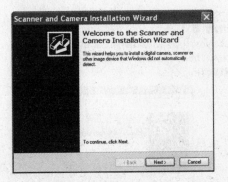

Fig. 4

Action 5

Select the manufacturer of the scanner or camera and then the model (Fig. 5).Click **Next**.

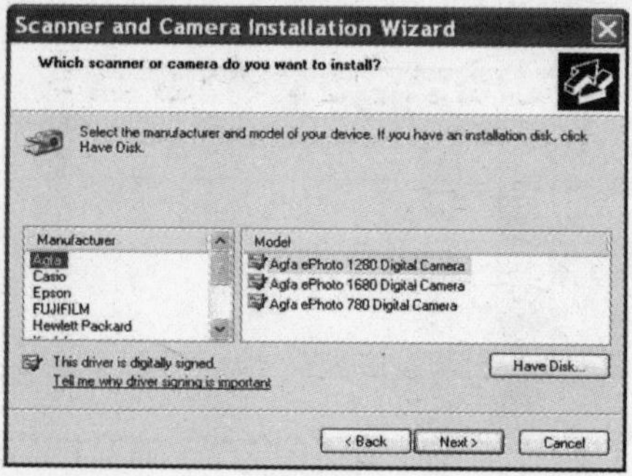

Fig. 5

Action 6

Select a port for your camera or scanner. If you are unsure which to choose, first try Automatic port detection. Click on **Next** (Fig. 6).

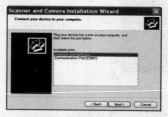

Fig. 6

Action 7

Confirm the name of your device. If the name of the camera or scanner is not correctly listed, then delete the existing name and type in the correct one (Fig. 7).

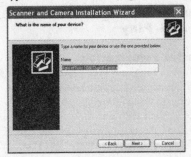

Fig. 7

Action 8

To complete the installation of the camera or scanner, click on **Finish** (Fig. 8).

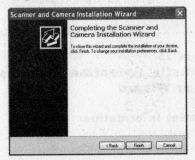

Fig. 8

Chapter Fourteen:
How to Add a Printer and Printing

Section 1:
Plug and Play

Essential Information

If you have a Plug and Play printer, Windows XP can usually automatically find and set up your printer without you needing to do anything. All you have to do is to plug in the printer's cable into the computer terminal and Windows will automatically install it for you. If this does not work, you will need to use the Add Printer Wizard.

Top Tip
Don't forget – you also need to connect your printer to mains power!

Section 2:
Automatic Detection with the Add Printer Wizard

Essential Information

The computer needs to be told that a printer has been attached and then it has to search through all of its systems to find it, key into it and make it operational. The **Add Printer Wizard** does all this automatically for you.

Action 1

Go to **Start**, and click on **Control Panel.** Click on **Printers and Other Hardware** (Fig. 1).

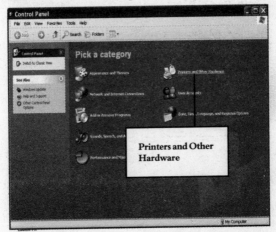

Fig. 1

Action 2

Click on **Add a printer**.

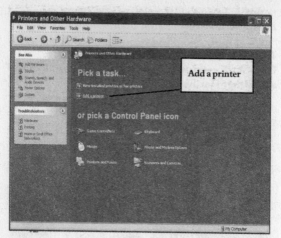

Fig. 2

Action 3

The **Add Printer Wizard** is displayed (Fig. 3). This will guide you through the process of adding the new piece of hardware.

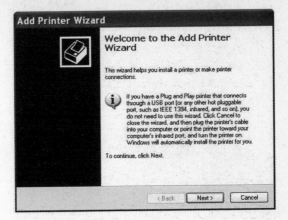

Fig. 3

Click on **Next**.

Action 4

Click the radio button that applies. If your computer is for
home or personal use and is not connected with another
computer, click on **Local printer**. Click on the check box
to enable the Wizard to automatically detect and install the
printer (Fig. 4).

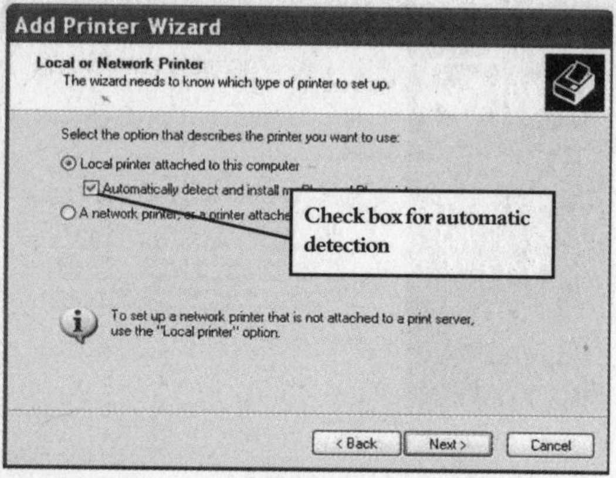

Fig. 4

Click on **Next**.

If the wizard is unable to find the printer, then you will need to install it manually. To do this, continue to Section 3.

Section 3:
Manual Detection with the Add Printer Wizard

Action 1
Follow all the steps for Section 2 but when you get to Figure 4 remove the tick from the check box by **Automatically detect and install my Plug and Play**

printer. Then click on **Next**.

Action 2

Select the correct port (Fig. 5). If you are unsure, then use the recommended port already listed. Click on **Next**.

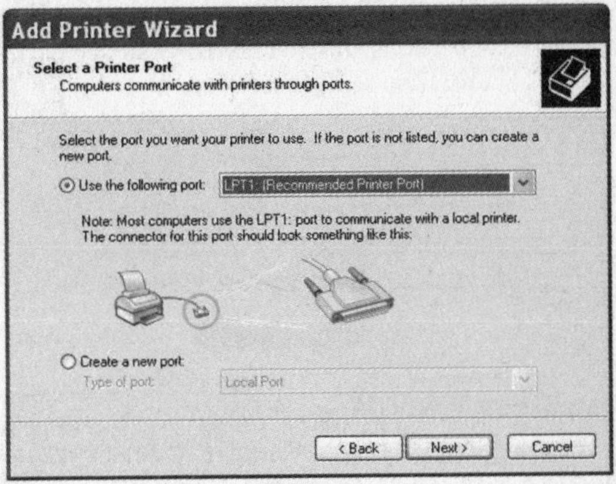

Fig. 5

Top Tip

If you make a mistake in your selection or change your mind, use the **Back** button to return to previous pages and make any alterations

---

Action 3

Select from the lists, the manufacturer and the name of your printer on the Wizard, (Fig. 6). The scroll bars will allow you to see more names.

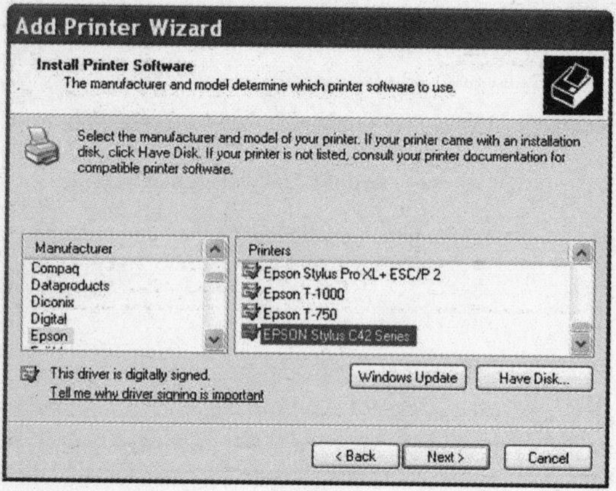

Fig. 6

Click on **Next.**

Action 4

The name should be automatically listed in the Printer name box. (Fig. 7).

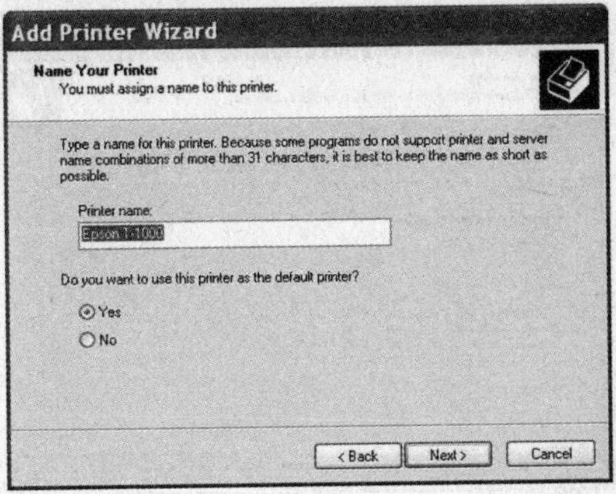

Fig. 7

If it is not, click in the box and type in the name. If this is
the only printer attached to you PC, also make sure the
Yes radio button is activated under **Do you want to use
this printer as the default printer?** Click **Next**.

Action 5
Make sure the radio button, **Do not share this printer,** is
activated (Fig. 8).

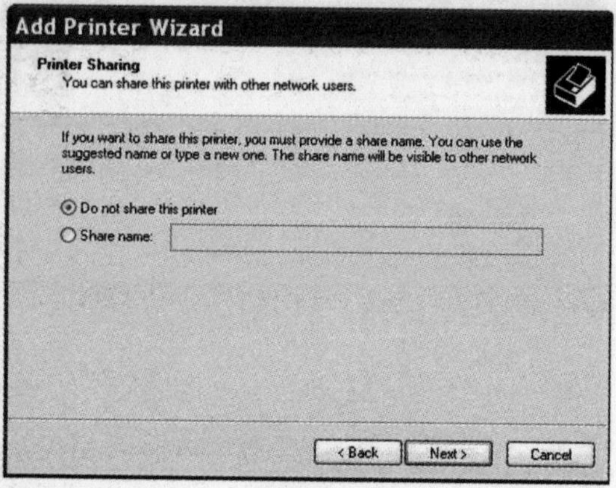

Fig. 8

Click **Next** and the **Print Test Page** dialogue box is displayed (Fig. 9).

Action 6

Once the printer is installed it is always a good idea to make sure that it prints. (Make sure that the printer is plugged into the mains and is switched on. Also check to see if your printer has an **On** button and if so, that it is switched on.) Click on the radio button of your choice and then click **Next**.

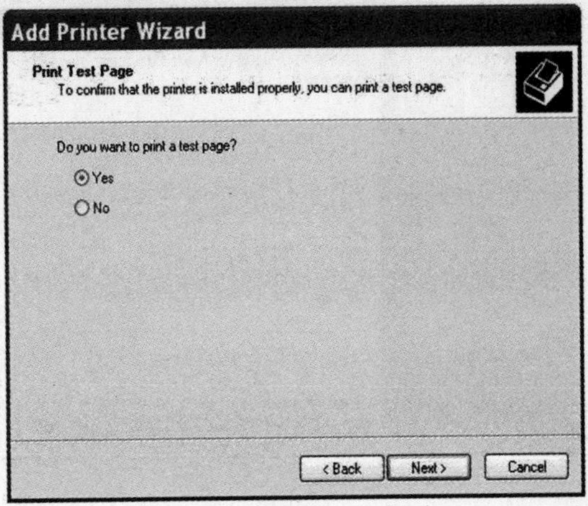

Fig. 9

Action 7

Read the list of settings on the Wizard and decide if you have made the correct selections. If you are happy with them, click on **Finish** and the Wizard will complete the setup.

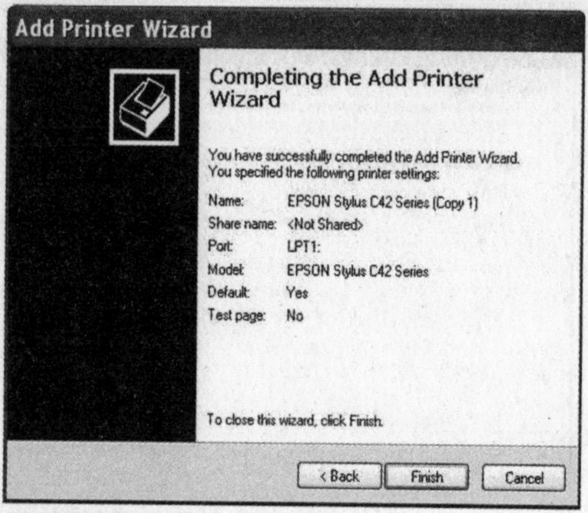

Add Printer Wizard

Completing the Add Printer Wizard

You have successfully completed the Add Printer Wizard. You specified the following printer settings:

Name: EPSON Stylus C42 Series (Copy 1)
Share name: <Not Shared>
Port: LPT1:
Model: EPSON Stylus C42 Series
Default: Yes
Test page: No

To close this wizard, click Finish.

[< Back]   [Finish]   [Cancel]

Fig. 10

Section 4:
Installing a New Printer Not Listed on the Wizard

Essential Information

You may at some point purchase a new model of printer which is not listed on the Wizard (Fig. 6). In this case follow all the actions up to Section 3 Action 3 but when you get to Figure 6, click on **Have Disk**. Insert the disk that accompanied the printer. Choose the drive and then click **OK**.

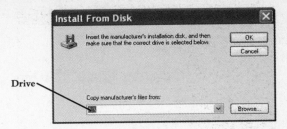

Drive

Fig. 11

Then follow the instructions as they appear on the screen.

Section 5:
Preparing to Print

Essential Information
Make sure that the printer is connected to the setup and that it is switched on and loaded with paper. Before printing you need to ensure that the computer knows what size of paper is being used and which way round the page should be. This is done through **Page Setup**.

Action 1
Go to **File** on the menu bar and click once. On the drop-down menu, click on **Page Setup** (Fig. 12).

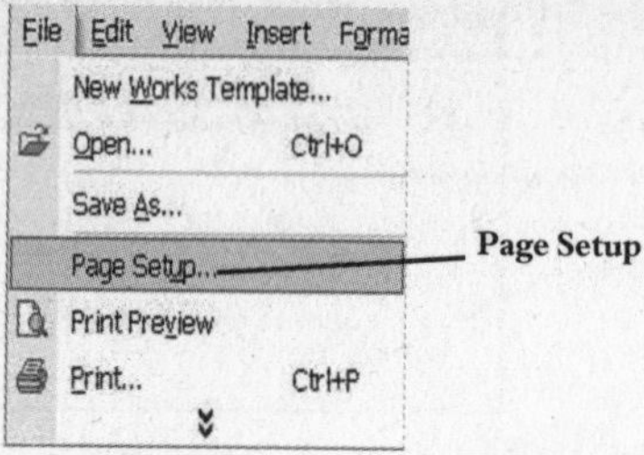

Fig. 12

Action 2

A box opens called **Page Setup** (Fig. 13). Notice that it has three tabs. Make sure that you select the tab called **Paper**.

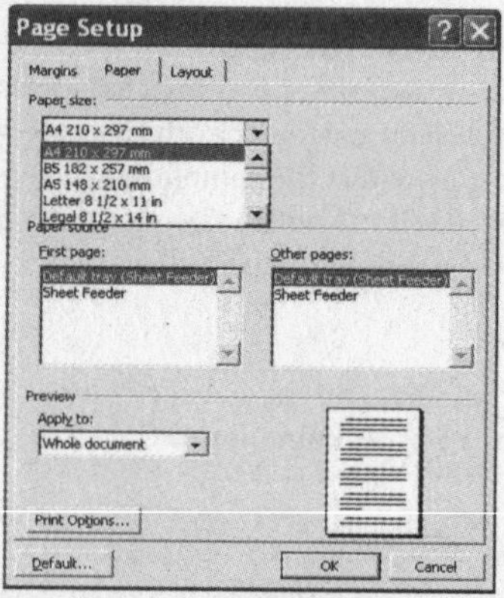

Fig. 13

Action 3

Under the title **Paper Size**, the text box has a down arrow. If you click on this a drop-down list will display the various paper sizes. For this exercise we will assume that you will be using A4 paper in your printer, so click on A4 210 x 297 mm.

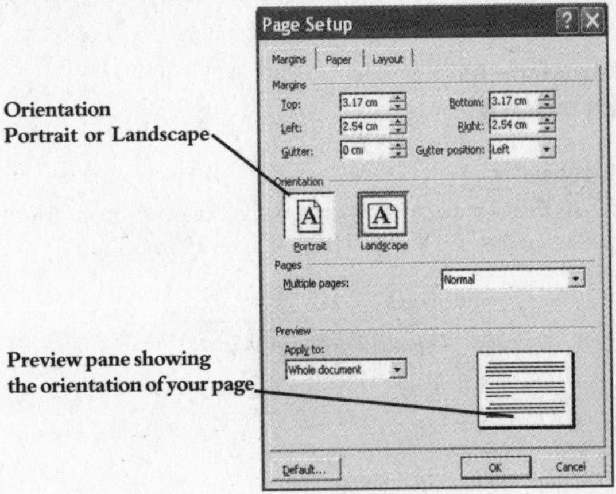

Orientation
Portrait or Landscape

Preview pane showing
the orientation of your page

Fig. 14

Action 4

In Figure 14 under **Orientation** you will see that you can choose whether to print in landscape or portrait. Click on the page displayed to choose **Landscape.** Notice also that a blue border is highlighted around your choice. Notice that the small preview page on the right of the page is in landscape style.

Now click on **Portrait.** The preview page has changed to a portrait style. This facility allows you greater flexibility in designing your documents.

Action 5
Now that you have completed the Page Setup you can go on to print.

Section 6:
Printing

Action 1
Go to **File** on the menu bar and click once. A drop-down menu appears (Fig. 15). Click once on **Print**.

File	Edit	View	Insert	Forma
New Works Template...				
Open...	Ctrl+O			
Save As...				
Page Setup...				
Print Preview				
Print...	Ctrl+P			

Fig.15

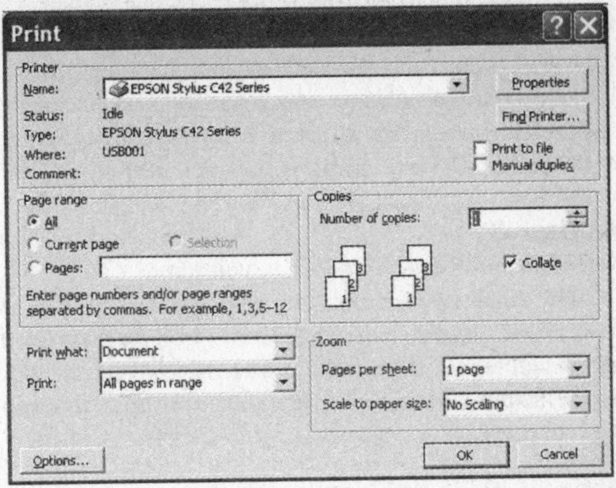

Fig. 16

Action 2

The **Print** dialogue box appears with various options (Fig. 16). Look at **Print Range**. You have a choice of what to print:

      All: If you choose this option all the pages of your document will be printed.

      Current Page: This option means that only the page that is currently visible on the screen will be printed.

      Pages: This option allows you to select certain pages within a document. When you choose this option you will need to type in the page numbers you wish to print in the pages text box. The printer

will then only print those pages that you have
selected.

When you have decided on which pages you wish to print,
click on the relevant radio button or type in the page range
in the text box. (For example 3, 5, 9 or 1–50.)

Action 3
Select the numbers of copies that you want.

The small upward pointing arrow will allow you to
increase the number in the copies box, whilst the downward
arrow will reduce the number. Alternatively you can click
on the text box and type in the number of copies that you
wish to print.

Action 4
Once you have selected the paper size, orientation and
number of copies, click on **OK** and the printing will begin.
If you change your mind and do not want to print at this
stage, click on **Cancel**.

Action 5
There is a printing shortcut on the Standard Toolbar fig 17.
It is the same picture of a printer found on the drop-down
menu from File. Only use this printer button when you
have already set up your page and only require one copy of
the document.

Standard

Print

Fig. 17

Section 7:
Printing from Outlook Express or Internet Explorer

Essential Information

The printing from Outlook Express or Internet Explorer is very similar to printing from a Word document except that the box that controls the printing is slightly different.

Action 1

For either Outlook Express or Internet Explorer click on File, then click on print.

Fig. 18

Outlook Express

Fig. 19

Internet Explorer

Action 2

The following window opens (Fig. 20). As you can see it is very similar to the previous print page but without the orientation capability.

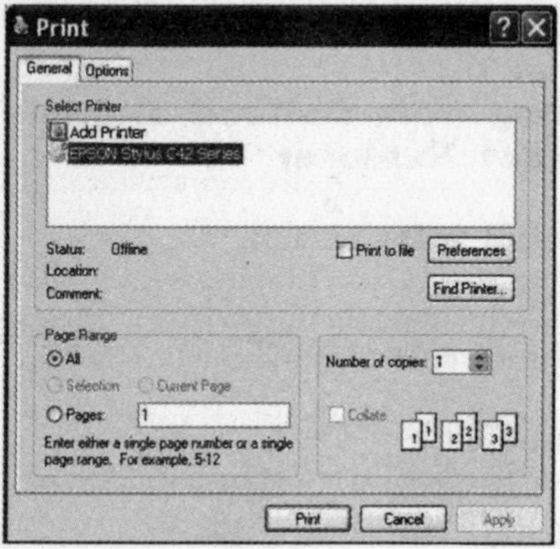

Fig. 20

Action 3

Click on the radio button to select to print 'All' pages in your document or select a Page range from the pages section.

Action 4

Click on the up or down arrows to select the number of copies that you want to print.

Action 5

Click on print.

Chapter Fifteen:
More on Windows

Section 1:
The Windows XP Tour

Essential Information
You can go on a Windows XP tour to discover more about
your PC. This can be done in stages or in one go, depending
on the time that you have available.

Action 1
Click on **Start**, **All Programs** and then **Accessories**.
Click on **Tour Windows XP**.

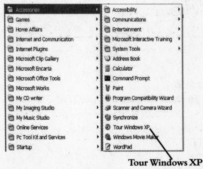

Tour Windows XP

Fig. 1

Action 2

The Welcome window opens. Select the format that you prefer by clicking on the radio button and then click **Next>** (Fig. 2).

Fig. 2

Action 2

Select a button to begin the tour (Fig. 3).

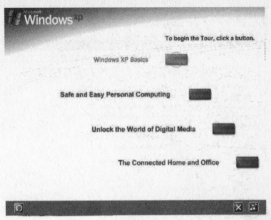

Fig. 3

Section 2:
Windows XP Interactive Training

Essential Information
The Interactive Training program will take you through
the exact steps to customise your PC and enable you to
learn more about the various programs.

Action 1
Click on **Start**, **All Programs** and then **Accessories**.
Click on Microsoft Interactive Training (Fig. 4).

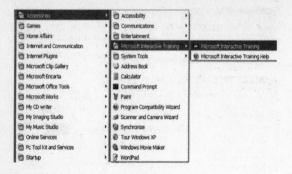

Fig. 4

Action 2

The **Select a Syllabus** box is displayed. If you have a home computer there will probably be only one syllabus listed. Click on **OK** (Fig. 5).

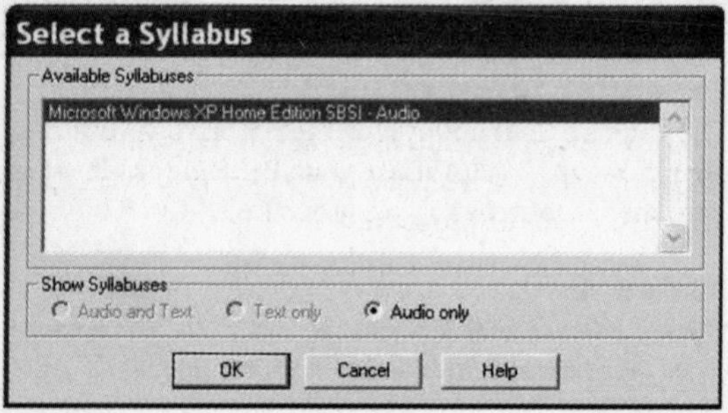

Fig. 5

Action 2

Click on the **green arrow** on the toolbar of the Course window to start the Interactive Training (Fig. 6).

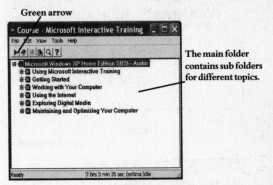

Green arrow

The main folder contains sub folders for different topics.

Fig. 6

Action 2

The Interactive window opens along with the 'controls' called **How to use this product**. The first lesson is on how to use these controls. As it is an interactive course, you will be prompted to respond at the appropriate time, and guided through the program.

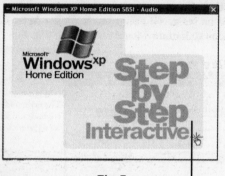

Fig. 7

Interactive window

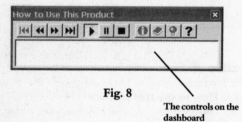

Fig. 8

The controls on the
dashboard

Section 3:
Calculator

Essential Information

The calculator can be either scientific or standard and works
in the same way as a hand-held calculator.

Action 1

Click on **Start, All Programs** and then **Accessories**.
Click on **Calculator** (Fig. 1).

Action 2

To change the view of the calculator, click on **View** and
select **Standard** or **Scientific** from the drop-down
menu, (Figs. 9 and 10).

Scientific view

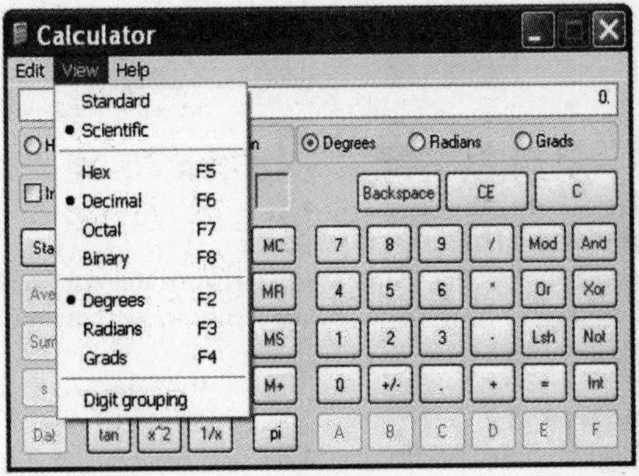

Fig. 9

Standard view

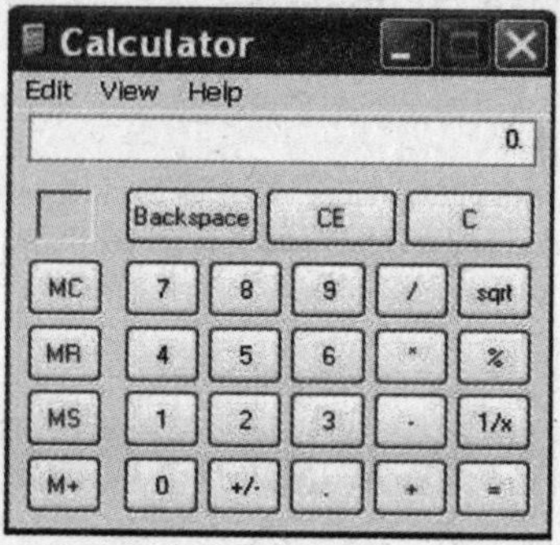

Fig. 10

Section 4:
Accessibility Options

Accessibility options allow users who have additional visual, hearing or mobility requirements to enhance and customise the computer.

Action 1

Click on **Start**, **All Programs** and then **Accessories** (Fig. 1). Click on **Accessibility** and then select from the drop-down menu (Fig. 11).

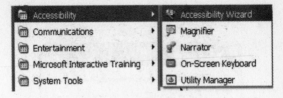

Fig. 11

The Magnifier
This enables you to select a magnification level and gives you tracking and presentation options.

Fig. 12

The Narrator
The Narrator can read aloud typed characters, commands

427

and announce events on screen (Fig 13). However it can only read in English.

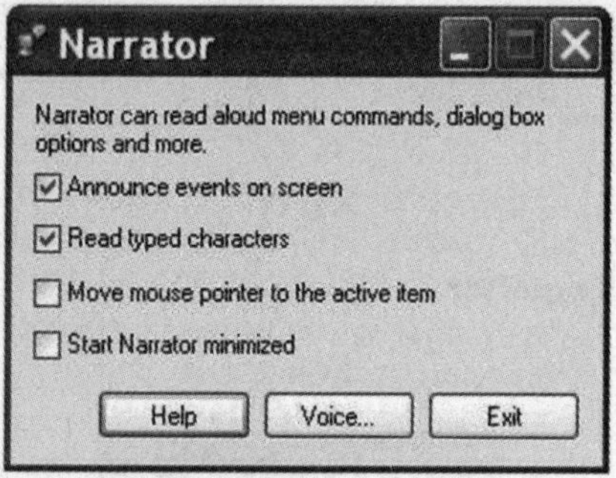

Fig. 13

The On-Screen Keyboard

The layout is the same as a traditional keyboard. The mouse pointer is used to operate the keys.

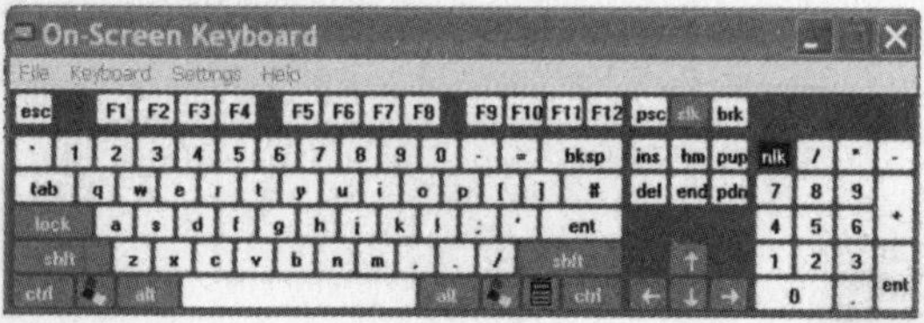

Fig. 14

Jargon Busters

backup

An extra copy of your data/programs.

BIOS

Stands for Basic Input/Output system. Permanently stored on the ROM chips inside the computer. Allows the computer to start.

bit

Short for Binary Digit. The smallest piece of information a computer can handle.

Broadband

Broadband requires a cable connection, rather than an overhead telephone line. A special box is fitted indoors to split the signal into telephone and Internet signals. It enables large amounts of data to be downloaded quickly and is almost three times faster than a dial-up connection.

byte

8 bits or approximately 1 character, i.e. a letter, space or number.

CD-ROM

Compact Disc- Read only Memory. A device storing

a large quantity of information that can be read by
any computer. Cannot be used for saving.

CD-R

Recordable CD can be used to store up to 650MB
of data.

CD-RW

A CD drive or player that will also write data onto
recordable CDs.

characters per second (cps)

The speed of printers is measured in characters
per second.

cheats

Articles, magazines or books written about how to
play certain games and the best way to win. They
are shortcuts to becoming more proficient.

chip

A silicon block holding thousands/millions of
transistors.

cookies

Small text files that are generated when you visit a
web site.

CPU

Central Process Unit. The main computer chip within the computer.

Cybercafé

Cafes that also have computers linked to the Internet and are available for public use for a small charge.

database

A type of program that organises sets of information.

defrag

Shorthand for defragmentation.

defragmentation

A process whereby a program within the computer rearranges the fragments of files which are stored on a number of places the hard disk. The pieces of each file are stored next to each other.

Dial-up

This uses the normal overhead telephone connections to access the Internet which has to be used separately to the telephone. You need to dial-up the ISP each time you wish to browse the web.

disk compression

A program that reduces the space that data takes up on the hard disk or floppy disk.

DOS

Disk Operating System. The most common operating system for IBM and compatible systems.

dot pitch

Measurement of how close dots are placed on the monitor. The closer the dots the better the image on the screen. Dot pitch is measured in millimetres.

dots per inch (dpi)

Measurement of the quality of a monitor or printer. The higher the number the better the quality.

download

The action of copying files from the internet onto your computer.

DVD

Stands for Digital Versatile Disk.

electronic mail (e-mail)

Messages sent from one computer to another over a network.

emoticons

Small pictures to convey emotions – used in
e-mails.

expansion slot

A slot at the rear of the computer that allows you to
add and connect electronic expansion cards or
boards to provide additional features to the
computer.

FTP

Stands for File Transfer Protocol. Process which
allows you to download and upload information as
files to and from the Internet.

FAQ

Frequently Asked Questions. Comes up on many
programs to help you get started.

floppy disk

3½" Floppy disk is a device capable of storing 1.3
MB (Megabytes) of information.

floppy drive

A slot in the front of the systems unit that takes a 3½"
floppy disk enabling data to be retrieved or saved.

font

Different typefaces/characters.

font size
Different sizes of the same font.

formatting toolbar
Enables text to be changed and moved.

freebies
Free software – available usually to download from the Internet.

game port
A connection at the back of the computer for a joystick/game pad etc.

Gb-RAM
The amount of Random Access Memory measured in Gigabytes.

gigabyte (Gb)
1 billion bytes.

gigahertz (Ghz)
The speed of your processor.

hard drive
The permanent PC storage device that holds programs and files measured in Mb or Gb (Megabytes or Gigabytes).

hardware

The physical components of the computer i.e. monitor, mouse, systems unit etc.

hertz (Hz)

Cycles per second used to measure frequency for monitors.

HTML

Stands for Hyper Text Mark up Language.

IAP

Internet Access Provider.

inkjet printer

A printer that sprays ink through tiny jets to create letters and characters.

Internet Café

As Cybercafés.

joystick

A joystick plugs into the game port at the back of the computer and is used to control games programs.

keyboard

A piece of computer hardware that allows communication between user and the computer.

kilobyte (K or KB)

1,024 bytes usually rounded down to 1,000 bytes.

laptop

A portable computer smaller than a briefcase.

laser printer

A printer that creates an image in the same manner as a photocopying machine.

local area network (LAN)

Two or more computers connected together via cables. The connected computers can share information, printers etc.

Mb-RAM

The amount of Random Access Memory measured in Megabytes.

megabytes

One million bytes. A byte is roughly 8 bits or one typed character. Memory is measured in megabytes.

megahertz (MHz)

The speed of the microprocessor is measured in Megahertz.

shareware

Software to download, usually free to use for a limited period, if you like it, you register your copy and pay a fee.

smilies

Another word for emoticons i.e. small pictures used to convey emotions – used in e-mails.

snail mail

The traditional postal service.

software

The programs within the computer.

sound card

A printed circuit board that handles and produces sounds. Plugs into expansion slots inside the systems unit.

spreadsheet

A program that handles number manipulation. Used for accounts, budgets and chequebook balancing.

systems unit

The box that holds all the electronic and electrical parts to make the computer work.

microprocessor

The main chip of the computer – its speed is measured in MHz or GHz.

millisecond (ms)

One thousandth of a second.

modem

Stands for Modulator and Demodulator. The modem changes a signal inside your computer to allow it to send and receive data over the telephone system.

monitor

TV screen that allows you to see your work. The size of the monitor is measured diagonally.

motherboard

The main printed circuit board that covers the base of the systems unit, enabling all the electronic components to connect with each other.

mouse

A device that controls the cursor arrow on the screen.

multimedia PC

A PC that is ready to be connected to the Internet. Would include CD-ROM drive, speakers and sound card enabling the computer to play video, graphics and sounds.

nanosecond (ns)
One billionth of a second.

newbie
A person who is new to the Internet.

operating system
The program that operates behind the scene telling the computer where to find files etc. The most common operating system for IBM compatibles is DOS.

palmtop
A hand-held computer.

parallel port
A connection at the back of the computer – most commonly used to connect a printer.

peripheral
Equipment that you connect to your computer i.e. game pad printer, scanner etc.

port
Ports are connections at the back of the systems unit. There are two types – serial and parallel.

processor
Main chip of the computer.

protocol
The rules and regulations that governs communications with the Internet.

RAM
Random Access Memory. Temporary storage space where data can be deleted or overwritten

ROM
Read Only Memory. Information that is permanently stored on chips within the computer. Cannot be overwritten.

scanner
The computer is able to copy an image placed onto the scanner. The image can then be viewed or used on documents.

search engines
Enormous directories built automatically by a computer program, which combs the Internet for information.

serial port
A connection at the back of the computer that transmits data.

virus

An unwanted piece of code attached to a program.
Can infect and corrupt programs within the
computer.

web directories

Organised logical lists based on a variety of
chosen categories. Each category is sub-divided
into further groups which are again sub-divided.

wizards

A mini program, which gives instructions and
information in given places thus leading you
through what could otherwise be a complex
procedure.

word processing program

Allows the user to create documents, letters, files,
memos etc.

Other Summersdale Titles

De-stress for Exams

£2.99 Paperback

You may have 101 textbooks about your chosen subject, but this is the only one you'll ever need on how to de-stress for your exams. Coping with stress while taking exams can be more testing than the papers themselves. *De-stress for Exams* will ensure you enter that exam hall with a clear head and a calm attitude – essential for tackling tests with the best possible chance of success.

Driving Test Tips

£2.99 Paperback

Don't let preparing for your driving test drive you up the wall!

With tips from instructors and new drivers alike for both before and during the exam, this little book is jam-packed with helpful advice to make sure that you feel in fine form for the open road… and that you lose your L-plates and not your cool.

Flying? No Fear!

Conquer your fear of flying

Capt. Adrian Akers-Douglas
and Dr George Georgiou

£2.50 Paperback

Written by an airline pilot and a clinical psychologist, this combination of practical explanation and self-help techniques is the definitive guide to help nervous passengers overcome their fear of flying.

Lighthearted, unpatronising and informative.

The Busy Body

Stress-free posture for
modern life

Penny Ingham and
Colin Shelbourn

£4.99 Paperback

The human body is not made for sitting at a desk for 40 hours a week. But when you're under pressure, the phone is ringing, there are faxes to send and meetings to attend, posture is the last thing you want to think about. Yet back pain is a problem for 49% of working adults and £6 billion is lost annually in time taken off.

This is the book we've all been waiting for. Offering easy, straightforward and, most importantly, effective solutions to posture problems, *The Busy Body* will change the way you stand, walk and sit, eliminating stiff necks and sore backs.

Written by a professional Alexander Technique teacher and fully illustrated, you'll wonder how your back survived before you read this book.

www.summersdale.com